5-
Minute
Baby
Animal
Stories

NATIONAL GEOGRAPHIC
WASHINGTON, D.C.

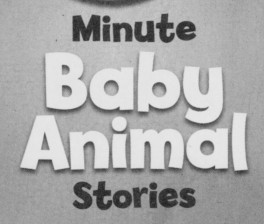

Contents

Learning at the Ape Academy 3

A Baby Sea Turtle's Journey 19

Ashima the Wolf Dog 37

Supercool Penguin Chicks 53

A Home for Baby Elephants 69

Hoot, Hoot, Hooray! 85

Wombat Rescue! 101

From Tiny Tadpoles
to Fabulous Frogs..................... 119

Jaguar Cub Cuties 137

Manatee Man to the Rescue 155

A Panda Cub Grows Up............ 173

A Baby Bobcat:
Lost Then Found 191

Learning at the Ape Academy

Budi sits on a wooden platform with other baby orangutans in a thick forest. A pile of leaf-covered branches sits in front of each small primate. Budi (pronounced BOO-dee) doesn't know what to do. He picks up a stick and looks at it. He plops the branch on his head. This is orangutan school, and it is time for today's lesson—how to build a nest. But why does an orangutan need to go to school?

Orangutans are the BIGGEST MAMMALS that live in trees.

In the wild, the mother would show her baby how to build a nest, which is where they would sleep each night. But Budi was separated from his mother shortly after he was born. For the first year of Budi's life, someone kept him as an illegal pet. He became very sick.

At first, Budi was so WEAK he couldn't OPEN HIS MOUTH.

Budi's owner called the International Animal Rescue in Kalimantan, Indonesia, for help. The conservationists took Budi to their rescue center. They took care of Budi and helped him get healthy.

Veterinarians at the center gave Budi orange slices to suck on. Budi liked those! The vets mushed up Budi's food and helped him to eat it.

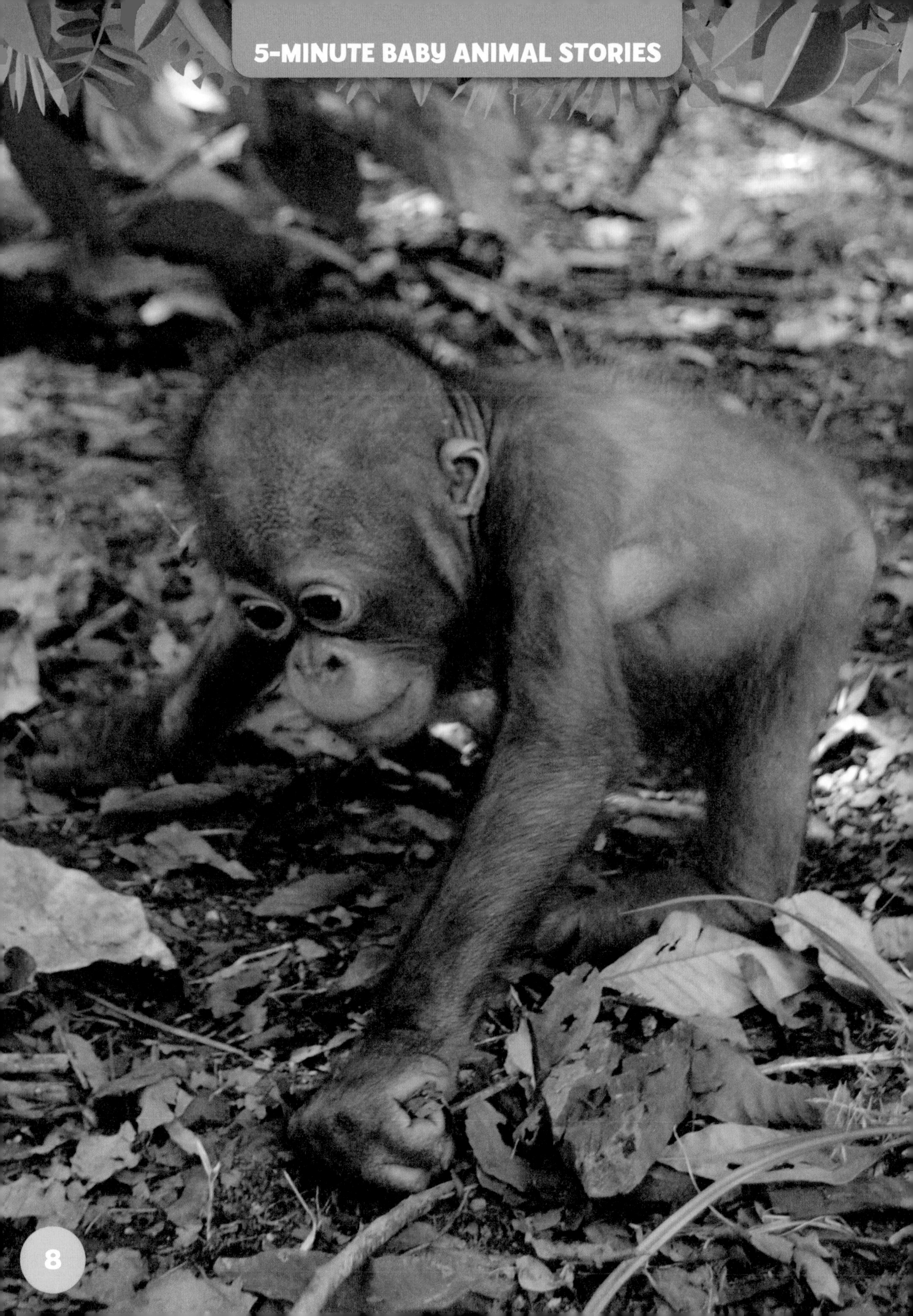

BUDI AND JEMMI (RIGHT)

Within a few weeks, Budi started to grab on to things to pull himself up. He learned how to climb in a tall enclosed tower filled with branches, small hammocks, rubber ropes, and rings.

Budi hadn't seen another orangutan since he lost his mother. Once he was healthy enough, volunteers introduced him to Jemmi, another orphaned orangutan.

Budi and Jemmi became best friends. They played together all day. They shared a hammock at night.

Soon it was time for school. Budi and Jemmi needed to meet other orangutans. And they needed to learn all the skills that orangutans must have to live in the forest.

BUDI AND JEMMI (BELOW)

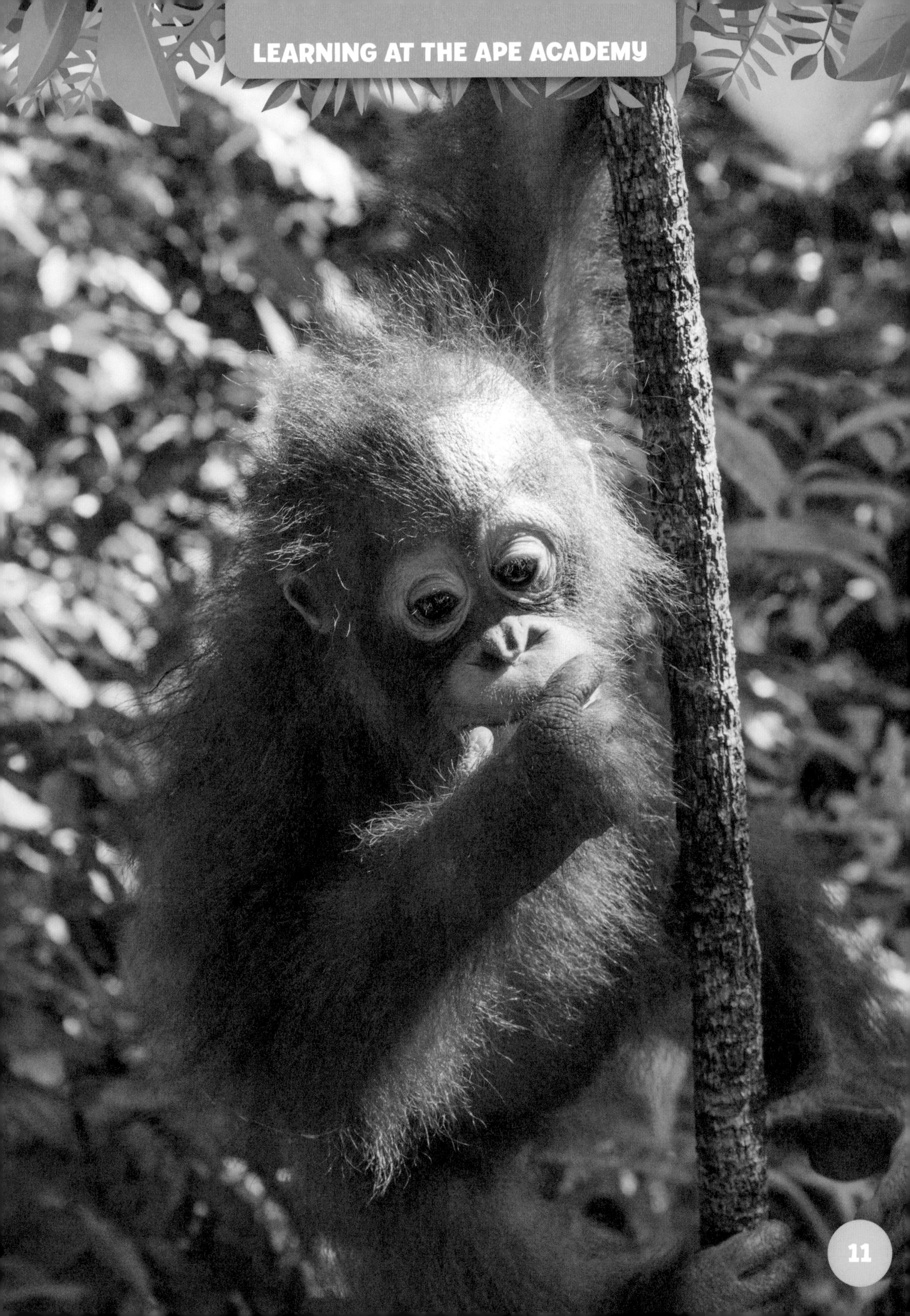

Step one was Baby School. Budi, Jemmi, and other orangutan orphans spent their days climbing and playing. Budi made new friends—he loved Baby School!

Budi and his classmates learned important lessons in the center's protected forest. One lesson was how to find food.

Orangutans have **LONG, CURVED FINGERS AND TOES**—perfect for **CLIMBING TREES!**

BUDI AND JEMMI (RIGHT)

Caregivers placed greens and fruit in different places. Sometimes the food was hidden in plain sight. Other times the students had to climb through a web of branches, rings, and rubber ropes to get it.

While Budi was in Baby School, he returned to the center to sleep at night. But one night, Budi refused to go back to his den. He wanted to spend the night in the forest.

Volunteers had also noticed that Budi no longer needed their help to do things. He was more confident and independent. Budi didn't want to share his nest with friends at night anymore, either. This was all good news! Budi was ready to graduate from Baby School.

As BUDI grew OLDER and STRONGER, he became a GREAT CLIMBER!

Two years after arriving at the center, Budi started Forest School. He lived with several other orangutans in the center's protected forest, learning the skills they'd need to survive in the wild.

Budi liked to climb to the tallest treetops. He hunted for rotten branches, where he could find a tasty termite meal!

Orangutans
must learn which
LEAVES TO EAT
and where to
find them.

Budi kept practicing his orangutan skills and exploring the treetops. The hope is that rescued orangutans like Budi will one day explore the trees outside of the Forest School, wild and free like they were meant to be. 🐾

A Baby Sea Turtle's Journey

Every two to three years, an adult female leatherback sea turtle goes on a journey. She swims back to a beach near where she hatched. She goes there to lay eggs of her own.

It is a very long trip. Sometimes that beach is across the ocean! If she is a first-time mother, she may not have been there for 15 years. But somehow

Instead of **HARD SHELLS, LEATHERBACKS** are covered with a layer of tough, **LEATHERY SKIN.**

She crawls up the beach until she is above the high-tide line. This will be a safe place for her eggs.

The mother digs a hole in the sand with her back flippers. This hole is her nest.

A leatherback egg is about the size of a BILLIARD BALL.

24

She lays eggs in the nest and covers them with sand. Then she returns to the ocean.

The nest is safe below the sand. It may hold up to a hundred eggs. The temperature of the sand covering a nest is important. It decides whether the turtles will be male or female. If the sand is cool, more males will hatch in the nest. If the sand is warm, more females will hatch.

For about two months, a baby turtle grows inside each egg. Then it begins *tap-tap-tapping* at its shell. To break the shell, it uses a special tooth called an egg tooth. The egg tooth falls out a few days later.

The baby wriggles from its broken shell. But it doesn't crawl out of the nest just yet. Instead, it waits until almost every egg in the nest has hatched. This can take up to seven days!

When all the babies are ready, they work together to dig out of the sand. Then one night, after dark, the babies pop up out of the nest all at once.

A BABY TURTLE is called a HATCHLING.

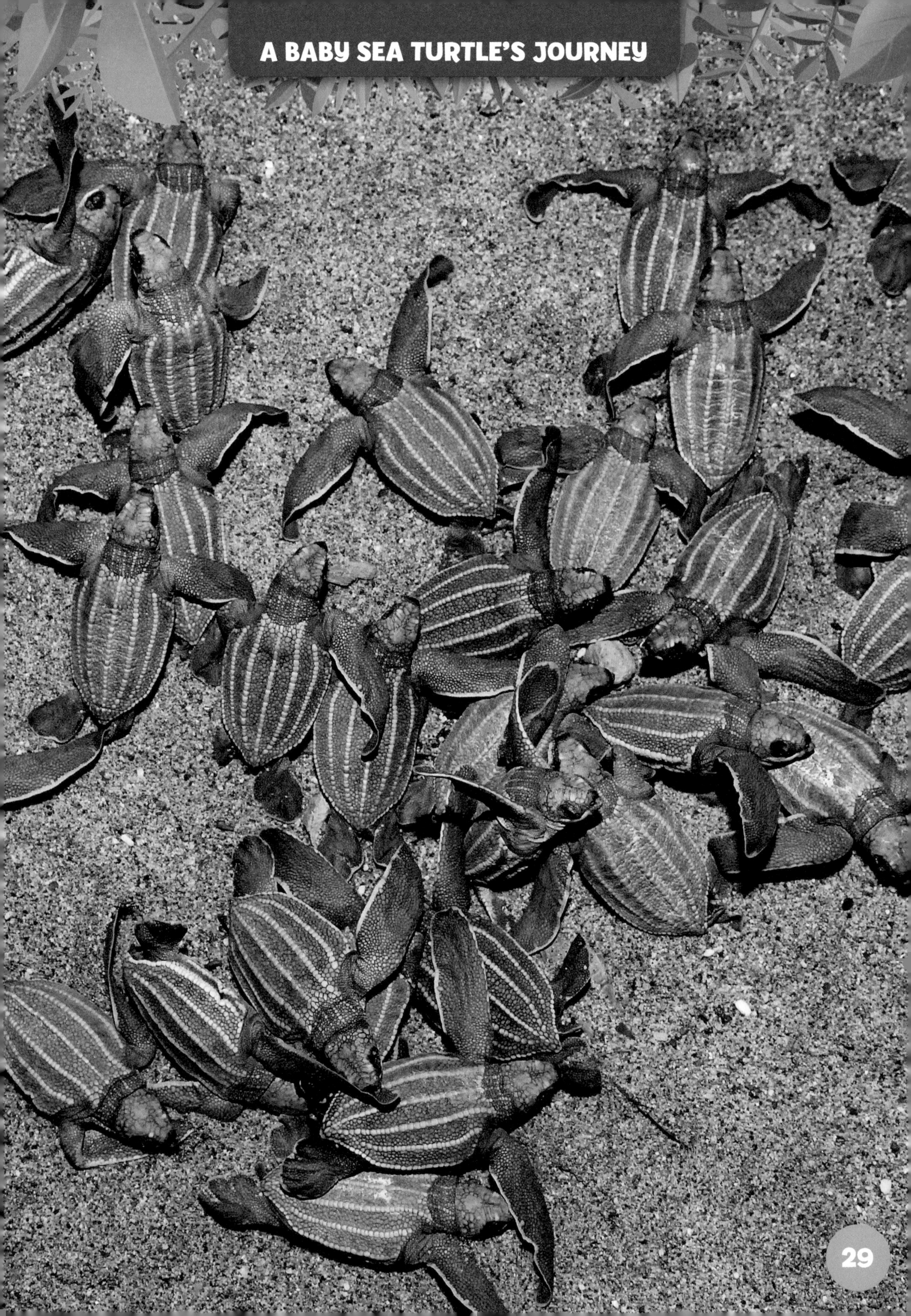

Traveling in a GROUP helps keep baby turtles SAFE FROM PREDATORS.

The moon shines in the sky. Its light reflects on the water. The baby leatherback sea turtles use the light and the downward slope of the beach to find their way to the ocean.

The race is on! The baby sea turtles crawl toward the water as fast as their tiny flippers will carry them. They need to reach the water before they get snatched up by hungry predators such as crabs, birds, foxes, and raccoons.

Once the baby turtles reach the ocean, they must swim through the waves crashing onto the beach. The little turtles must also stay away from hungry predators in the water. Dangers are everywhere!

The baby turtles rush to reach open water, far from the shore. They swim to clumps of seaweed that float far out in the ocean.

Leatherback sea turtles can LIVE FOR MORE THAN 50 YEARS.

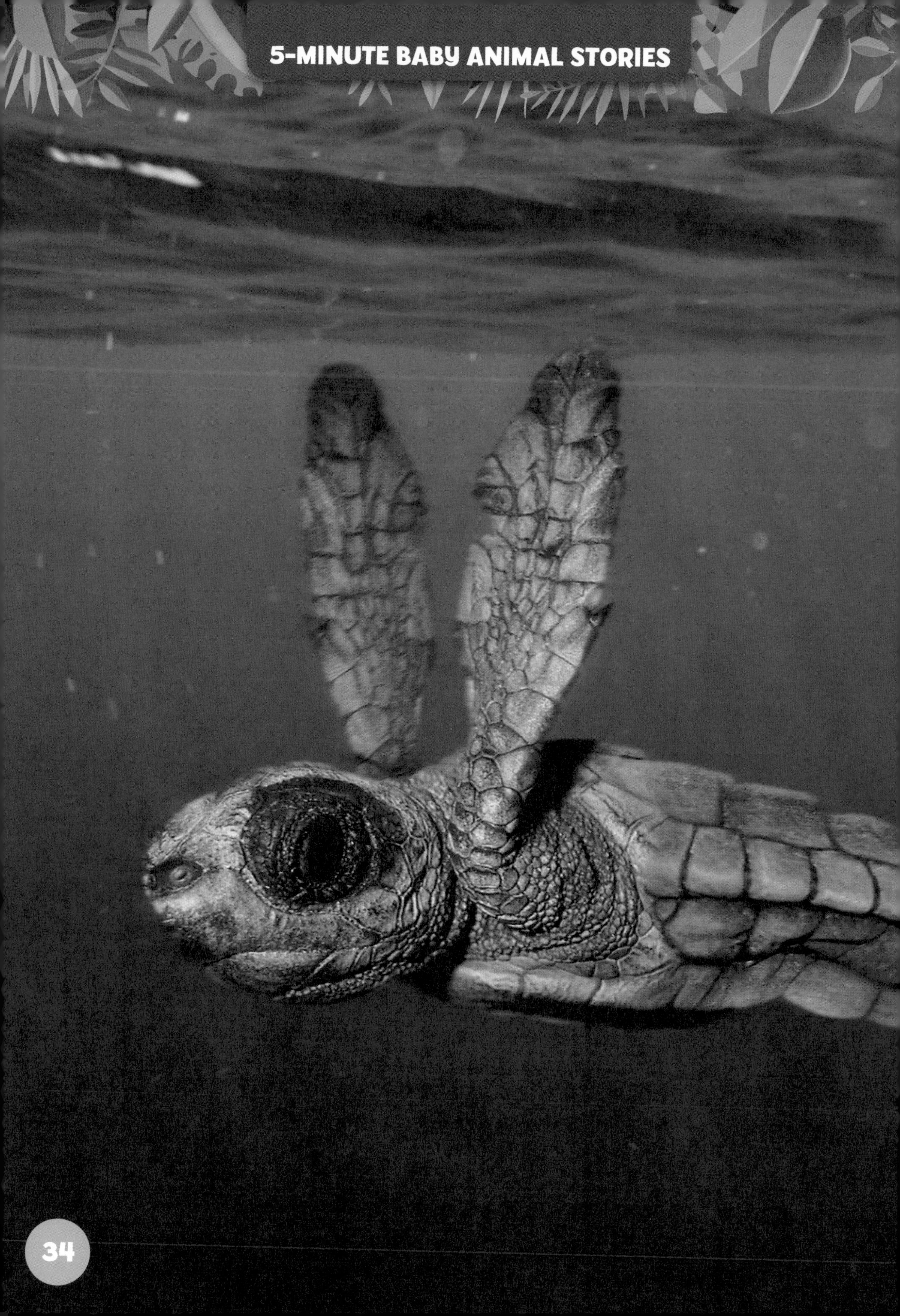

The babies stay in the seaweed for several years. They gobble plants and tiny sea animals. They hide from predators. This is a safe place for them to live and grow.

And grow is exactly what they do! Before long, the babies are the size of dinner plates. It is time to leave the open ocean.

The young sea turtles swim to shallow waters closer to the coast. There's lots of food to eat here. It is a good place for a sea turtle to grow into an adult.

Someday the female turtles will go back to a beach near where they hatched. They will lay their own eggs, and the journey will start all over again. 🐾

Ashima the Wolf Dog

On a spring day, a litter of pups was born in a backyard in Colorado, U.S.A. They were wolf dogs, which are part wolf and part dog. One of the pups was a female with soft black fur. The owners named her Storm.

When Storm was three weeks old, a young couple bought her. They thought Storm would be a great buddy for their three-year-old German shepherd. She wasn't, though. The thing is, wolf dogs aren't like regular dogs, and they shouldn't be kept as pets.

When Storm was nine weeks old, she got into a fight with the German shepherd. Storm's back right leg was badly broken. The couple took her to their veterinarian. She needed an operation. After the surgery, Storm's leg was still in bad shape.

STORM couldn't live with a broken leg. IT HAD TO BE FIXED.

Storm's new owners knew they couldn't raise her properly. Regular rescue centers couldn't care for a wolf dog, either. So the couple called W.O.L.F. That stands for Wolves Offered Life and Friendship. It's a rescue center, or sanctuary, that helps wolf dogs and gives them a home for life.

The **W.O.L.F. SANCTUARY** can care for 30 wolves and wolf dogs.

Michelle, W.O.L.F.'s director of animal care, took Storm to the doctor. Storm needed another surgery, but she wasn't strong enough yet.

There was another problem. The wolf dogs at the sanctuary live in packs—a lot like wolves in the wild. But Storm was still healing, and she was too young to live with a pack. So Michelle took Storm home with her. She and her sister, Christy, would look after the pup.

At Michelle's house, Storm ran, jumped, climbed, and chewed everything she saw. Michelle put baby gates in doorways. Storm climbed over them. Michelle put up higher gates. Storm climbed over those, too!

Michelle didn't think Storm was the right name for this fearless pup. The people at W.O.L.F. decided to call her Ashima, after Ashima Shiraishi, one of the world's best rock climbers. "Ashima" means "without boundaries" in Hindi and Sanskrit. The name was perfect!

If they become bored, wolf dogs might DESTROY THINGS or try to ESCAPE THEIR enclosures.

Ashima's second operation was a success. But she couldn't run or jump for at least four weeks. Michelle kept Ashima in a dog crate to keep her still. Ashima didn't like it. She quickly figured out a way to be let out: If she peed or pooped, then Michelle or Christy *had* to let her out so they could clean the crate. If Ashima rolled in the mess, she got a bath. That took even longer!

Michelle started taking Ashima on walks. When they saw squirrels, Ashima didn't bark and chase them like most dogs would. She crouched low, placed one paw in front of the other, and inched forward. She acted just like a wolf!

47

ASHIMA was known at W.O.L.F. for being a "WILD CHILD"!

A month later, the doctors removed the stitches from Ashima's leg. They x-rayed it. Good news! The leg was stronger. It moved well. And it was growing just like Ashima's other legs.

Ashima needed to stay calm for three more weeks. But the pup wasn't ready to live with the other wolf dogs. And Michelle couldn't keep her at home any longer. So Ashima got a new home at the W.O.L.F. sanctuary. Staff members took turns watching the pup day and night.

At the sanctuary, Ashima smelled pine trees. She heard leaves rustling, birds singing—and other wolf dogs howling! Her tail thumped with excitement.

Ashima had a lot of energy, so Michelle gave her a job. She put down art canvases and animal-safe paints. Ashima stomped and smeared paint on the canvases. She rolled in the paint, too! Michelle sold Ashima's creations to raise money for the sanctuary.

WOLF DOGS can jump six feet (1.8 m) into the air!

ASHIMA AND SPARTACUS (RIGHT)

By late summer, Ashima's leg had healed. It was time to become part of a pack. Sanctuary workers introduced her to Spartacus, a six-year-old male wolf dog. Spartacus is an "ambassador" animal. He teaches people about wolf dogs. Ashima and Spartacus quickly became best buddies.

Michelle thought Ashima would make a good ambassador, too. She was right! Ashima and Spartacus worked together well.

Ashima grew to become a happy and healthy wolf dog. The rescue center gave her just what she needed—a safe place to live, other wolf dogs to play with, and people who cared about her. 🐾

Supercool
Penguin Chicks

It is April in Antarctica and winter is coming. Emperor penguins burst out of the Southern Ocean. They have fattened up after a summer of feasting on fish, krill, and squid in the sea.

Emperor penguins can LEAP OUT OF THE WATER up to six feet (1.8 m) in the air.

Winter in Antarctica lasts for six months. Temperatures drop to minus 76°F (-60°C). Blizzards bring winds that blow up to 124 miles an hour (200 km/h). For part of the winter, darkness covers the snowy, icy land 24 hours a day. For emperor penguins, this is the perfect time and place to raise a baby!

Some **PENGUIN COLONIES** have up to 40,000 **BIRDS!**

Before they can do that, the emperors must reach their colony, which is the group of penguins they stick with. They waddle or slide on their bellies across the ice. The colony may be up to 75 miles (120 km) away.

Once they arrive at the colony, the male penguins pair up with female penguins.

By June, each female penguin lays one egg. The mother penguin gives the egg to the father penguin. Then she returns to the sea so she can fill her hungry tummy.

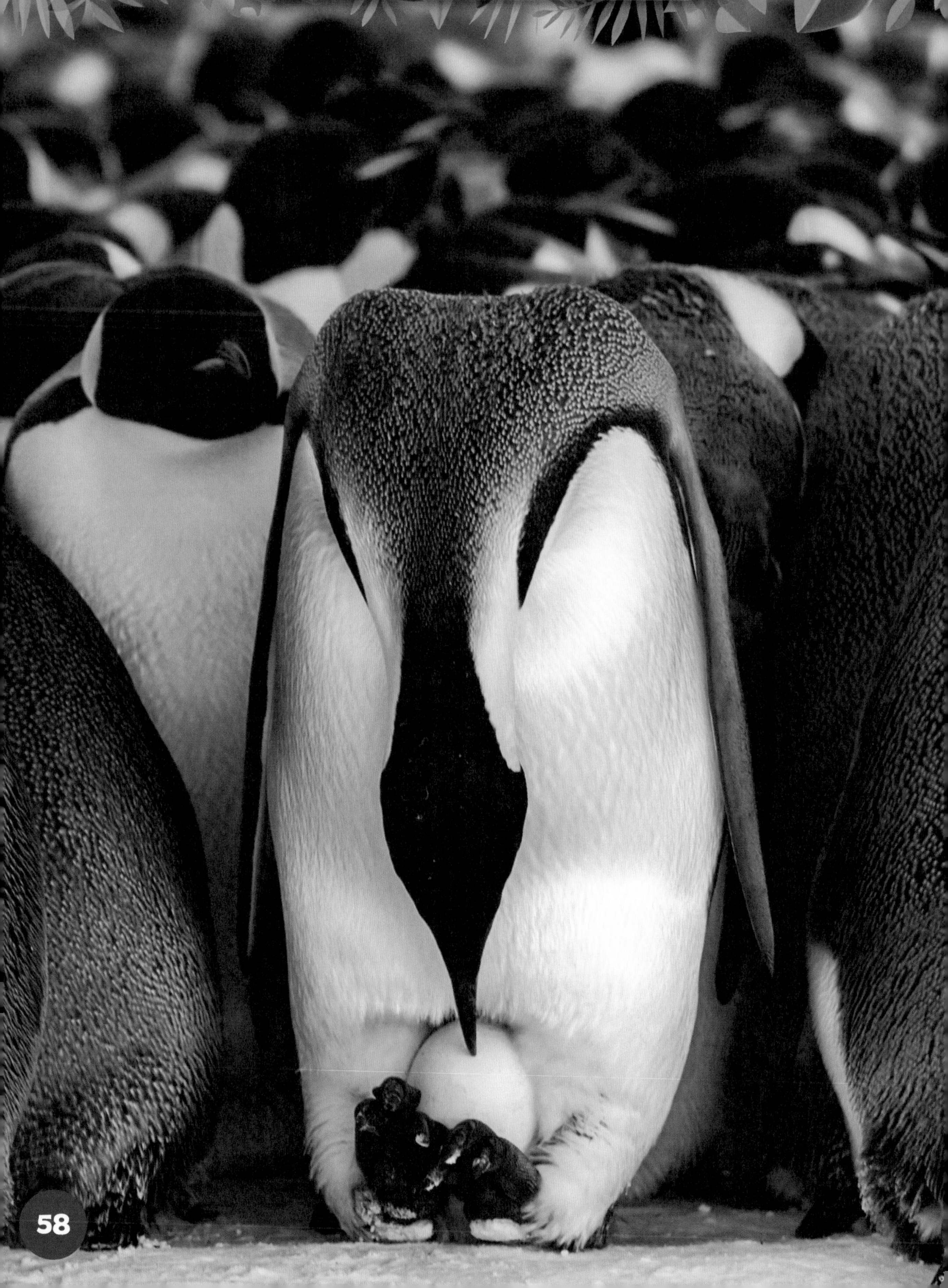

The father penguin stays put. It's his job to take care of the egg. In Antarctica, that is a challenge. If an egg touches the icy ground, it will not survive.

So the father penguin balances the egg on his feet. He presses the egg up against a bare flap of skin called a brood pouch. Then he covers the egg with his feathered skin. For the next two months, he stands in darkness. He does not eat. To keep warm, he huddles together with other fathers.

Finally the female penguins return. They call for their mates. Even in a huge colony, emperor penguin parents recognize one another's special call.

When a female penguin reaches her mate, the father carefully transfers the egg to the mother's feet. Then he heads out to sea to find food. He is very hungry!

The mother penguin's timing is perfect. The egg is ready to hatch. *Peep, peep!* A little chick breaks out of its shell. It's hungry! Mom regurgitates, or throws up, food for the chick to eat.

The baby penguin has a black-and-white face. Its body is covered with soft, fluffy silver feathers. Just like the egg, the newly hatched chick must sit on a parent's feet to stay warm. The chick will freeze in just a few minutes if it touches the ice.

Emperor penguins can stay UNDERWATER for more than 20 MINUTES!

The emperor penguin parents take turns caring for their fast-growing baby. One parent stays on land, caring for the chick. The other parent rushes to the ocean for more food to regurgitate for the baby.

In August and September, the colony is alive with noise and activity. Hungry chicks chase parents returning from the sea. They want food! But an emperor parent will only feed its own chick. Parents call their chicks, and chicks call their parents. They recognize each other's calls. It's time to eat!

By October, the chick can stand on the ice by itself. Now both parents go to the ocean to fish at the same time. They return to the colony less and less. The chick stays with a group of other young chicks while they are gone. The chicks huddle together. This keeps them warm and safe.

Soon the chick begins to molt, or shed its fluffy baby feathers. It then grows black and white water-proof feathers. Molting takes about two months. The young penguin does not eat this entire time.

By December, summer in Antarctica is starting. Warmer temperatures melt the ice along the shores and cause it to break up.

A group of **PENGUIN CHICKS** living together is called a **CRÈCHE.**

ZZZ ZZZ

The chicks are finally ready to dive into the ocean on their own. With their new waterproof feathers, they can swim and catch fish for themselves. With a splash, they leave the ice and begin to explore the watery world below. 🐾

A Home for Baby Elephants

A scared baby elephant stood near her mother in a dry wilderness in Kenya. The mother elephant was badly hurt. She had been shot by poachers—people who hunt animals illegally.

The baby, called a calf, was only 18 months old. She still needed her mother to give her milk and to protect her from lions and other hungry predators. But her mother was too weak.

Scouts on patrol from a nearby ranch found the two elephants. They immediately contacted the Kenyan Wildlife Service and a conservation group called the Sheldrick Wildlife Trust. The Trust had mobile veterinary units—vehicles that carry all the medicines and supplies needed to treat wounded animals. One unit rushed to the scene.

The rescuers tried very hard, but they could not save the mother elephant. They were heartbroken. But there was one bright spot. The calf seemed to be OK!

Rescuers wrapped the young elephant in a blanket. She was very upset, so they gave her medicine to help her relax. The medicine made the calf tired. She fell asleep.

Just like humans, animals need REST TO HEAL.

The rescuers lifted the sleeping calf into a truck. She was heavy—700 pounds (318 kg)! The team drove her to a nearby airfield and loaded her onto a plane. The plane took her to Nairobi, Kenya. The calf was weak and dehydrated. During the flight, the team gave her special liquids through a tube. The liquids helped the baby elephant grow stronger.

After the plane landed, the young elephant was moved to the Trust's nursery.

In the nursery, there are other orphaned elephants and rhinos. People there take great care of the babies, making sure they have what they need to get healthy.

When babies first come to the Trust, they are often weak and hungry. In the wild, a baby elephant drinks its mother's milk for the first few years of its life. At the Trust, the babies are given big bottles of milk every three hours, day and night.

Just a few months after they're born, baby elephants begin to eat plants, too. They use the tips of their trunks to pull leaves off of trees and grass from the ground. Yum!

76

Angela Sheldrick, head of the Trust, and the other caretakers work hard to help the babies feel safe and calm. They feed the animals and care for them. At night, they will even sleep inside the elephants' enclosures. This helps the babies feel less alone.

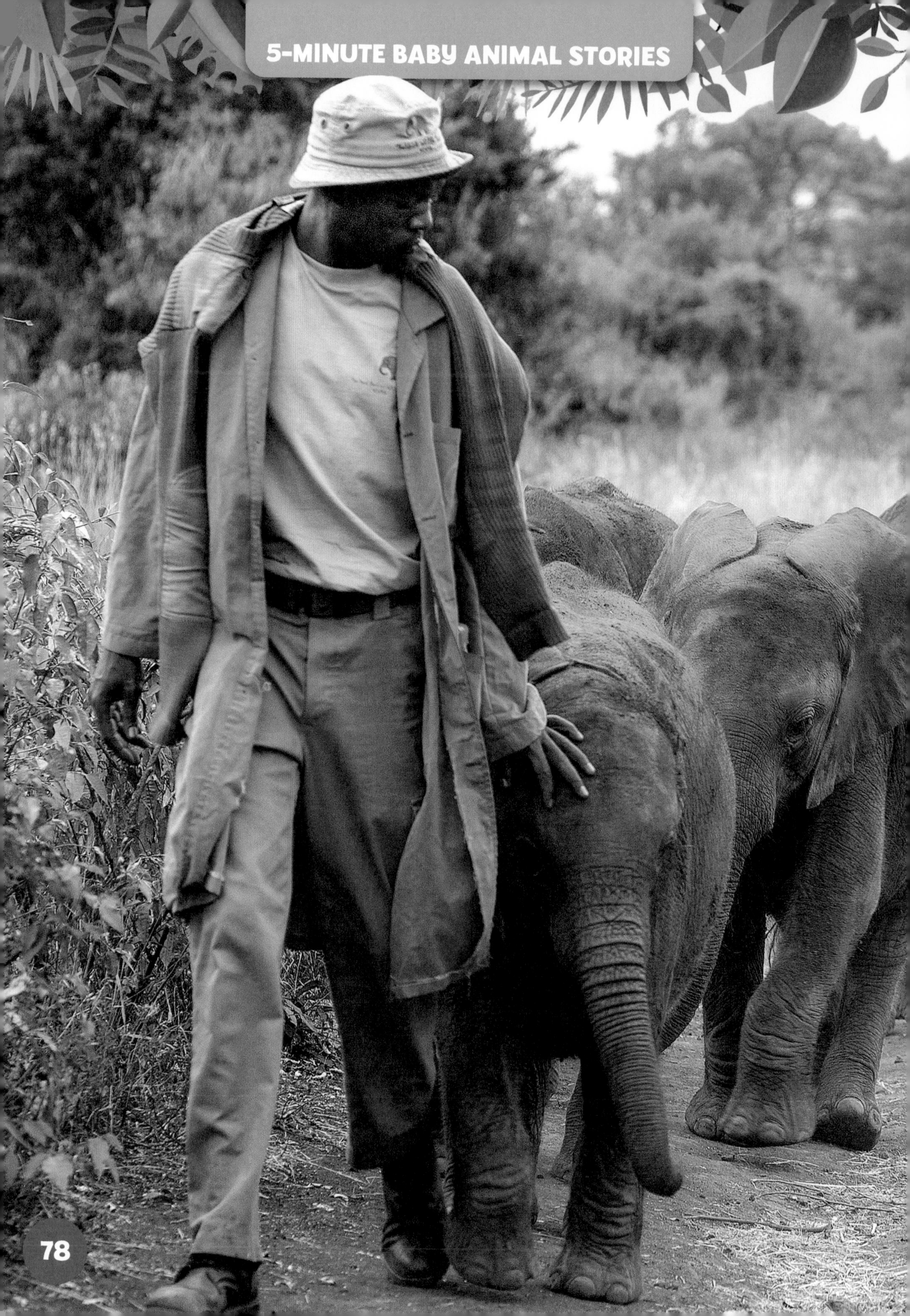

Every day, the young elephants go for a walk together. Keepers lead them through the nearby forest. In the wild, a baby learns how to be an elephant by watching its mother and older family members. At the Trust, the caretakers do their best to teach them the skills they need.

79

An **ELEPHANT'S TRUNK** has about **40,000** **MUSCLES.**

Another great way for baby elephants to learn is by hanging out with the herd. They learn to munch on leaves and grass, just like the older elephants do. They also practice using their long, floppy trunks to feed themselves.

The baby elephants make friends with other elephants at the nursery. They spend their days rolling in dirt, splashing in water holes, and chasing dragonflies. Young elephants love to play. Sometimes they will push and play fight, and other times they will toss a branch from a tree up into the air.

When orphaned elephants become big enough, they may be introduced to a wild elephant herd. It's likely that some of the elephants that were raised together will stay best friends once they're living in the wild.

Elephants **COVER THEIR SKIN** in **DUST** and **MUD** to protect it from the sun!

While at the Trust, the baby elephants enjoy their playtime and their pals, both human and elephant. They get healthy and strong and learn a lot. One day they'll be ready to return to where they belong—the wild. 🐾

AFRICAN ELEPHANTS are the LARGEST land animal ON EARTH!

BARRED OWL

Hoot, Hoot, Hooray!

GREAT GRAY OWL

High up in a pine tree, a mother owl is tidying a nest to lay her eggs. She will lay between one and 14 white, oval eggs. Then she will lay her body on top of the eggs to keep them warm. This is called incubation. During this time, the mother owl loses some of the feathers on her belly, so she can press her bare skin to the eggs. This keeps the eggs nice and toasty.

The mother owl sits on the eggs for three to five weeks until the baby owls, called owlets, hatch from their shells. Welcome to the world, baby owls! The adorable owlets are covered in a short, fluffy layer of feathers called down.

BARN OWL

The GROUP OF EGGS laid by a female owl is called a CLUTCH.

87

Owlets are born with their eyes closed, and until they open several days later, the baby owls can't see. For the first few weeks of their lives, they can't fly or even keep themselves warm. Thankfully, the mother owl is there to keep her owlets safe. She snuggles the hatchlings underneath her.

EURASIAN EAGLE OWL AND OWLETS

BARRED OWL OWLET

Though owls are good at many things, making a nest is not one of them. So, instead of making their own, many owls use nests that were built by other birds or by squirrels. Different kinds of owls make homes in barns, in holes in trees, or even in underground burrows.

ELF OWL OWLETS

Some species of owlets can **EAT THREE OR FOUR MICE** per night.

Some owls make their home in the middle of a field. And others find a way to get cozy in the prickliest of places—a cactus!

When it's time to eat, the father owl catches food and brings it back to the nest for the mother and the owlets. Different types of owls eat all sorts of different things. Some owls eat rodents, like mice and voles. Other owls eat frogs, lizards, or snakes.

LITTLE OWLS

There are about 250 different owl species. They range from the teeny tiny to the large and mighty. Bigger owls, like the great horned owl, might eat rabbits, squirrels—even skunks! Smaller owls, like the elf owl, the tiniest in the world, eat only insects.

GREAT GRAY OWL OWLET

GREAT GRAY OWL AND OWLET

Owls are great hunters. They have special skills—such as super hearing—that help them find and catch their prey. We can't see an owl's ears, but they're there, hidden below the feathers around its head. Some owls have such good hearing that they can find and catch a small animal scurrying underneath the snow!

BARN OWL AND OWLETS

Many owls SWALLOW THEIR PREY WHOLE.

Most owls are nocturnal. This means they sleep during the day and stay awake during the night. That's when nocturnal owls hunt, so it's a good thing that they can see well in the dark!

When owls want to look at something, instead of moving their eyes from side to side, they move their whole head. And they can turn their head almost all the way around! Whoa! That's cool!

BURROWING
OWL FLEDGLING

95

Rather than FLAP THEIR WINGS, owls mostly GLIDE.

SHORT-EARED OWL

Besides their keen hearing, another thing that makes owls expert hunters is that they can fly super-duper quietly. They have special wings and feathers that help them to fly slowly and with almost no sound! *Shhh!* This means owls are very good at sneaking up on their prey!

To catch their prey, owls use their long, curved, razor-sharp claws, called talons. When a father owl brings a meal back to the nest, the mother owl tears it into small pieces to feed the babies, beak-to-beak.

LITTLE OWL AND OWLET

When baby owls are a few weeks old, they begin to leave the nest for little adventures, exploring the area nearby. Sometimes they will even hide in bushes or tall grass.

PHARAOH EAGLE OWL OWLETS

BURROWING OWL
FLEDGLING

A few weeks later, the little owls begin to learn to fly. At this stage, they are called fledglings. As the owls grow bigger, they begin to develop their talons and sharp, round beaks. Their fluffy down is replaced with grown-up feathers. Soon they reach their full size.

It's time now for the young owls to leave the nest and live on their own. There's a great big beautiful world just waiting to be explored! 🐾

Owls are **MEMBERS** of a **GROUP OF BIRDS** called **RAPTORS.**

EURASIAN EAGLE OWL

Wombat Rescue!

ZZZZ_z

Z Z_z

One dark night, a man driving down a busy highway in Australia saw something on the side of the road. It looked like a wombat. The driver stopped to see if he could help it. Sadly, it had been hit by another car. He could not help it. But wait …

NEXT 96 km

FEMALE WOMBATS give BIRTH TO ONE JOEY every two years.

Wombats are marsupials, like kangaroos. They carry their babies, called joeys, in their pouches. The man knew the pouch opened toward the mother's rear instead of her head. That's how she keeps dirt out when digging. He looked inside. He saw a tiny, clawed paw. Suddenly it moved. The joey was alive!

The man rushed the young wombat to a nearby wildlife caregiver. The baby seemed healthy, but he was only about five months old. In the wild, wombats stay with their mothers for up to two years. This baby probably hadn't spent much time outside of his mother's pouch. It would be a long time before he could live on his own.

JOEYS drink their MOTHER'S MILK even after they LEAVE THE POUCH.

The joey was taken to the Goongerah Wombat Orphanage in southeast Australia. Its founder, Emily Small, named him Bronson. She was his new human foster mom. Emily was already taking care of another male joey named Landon. Like Bronson, Landon had lost his mother in a car accident. Both babies had survived wildfires, too.

It takes a lot of work to foster a baby wombat. Emily decided to take the joeys home with her.

Emily wrapped the joeys in blankets and cuddled them a lot. This made them feel like they were safe inside their mothers' pouches. She laid them in small, soft cat beds with heating pads. The joeys were warm and comfy.

Emily bottle-fed the babies up to five times a day. She used a mixture similar to their mothers' milk.

After the joeys ate, they roamed the apartment. Their claws clicked on the floor as they moved. Sometimes the clicking stopped—and Emily knew one of the babies was eating something he shouldn't!

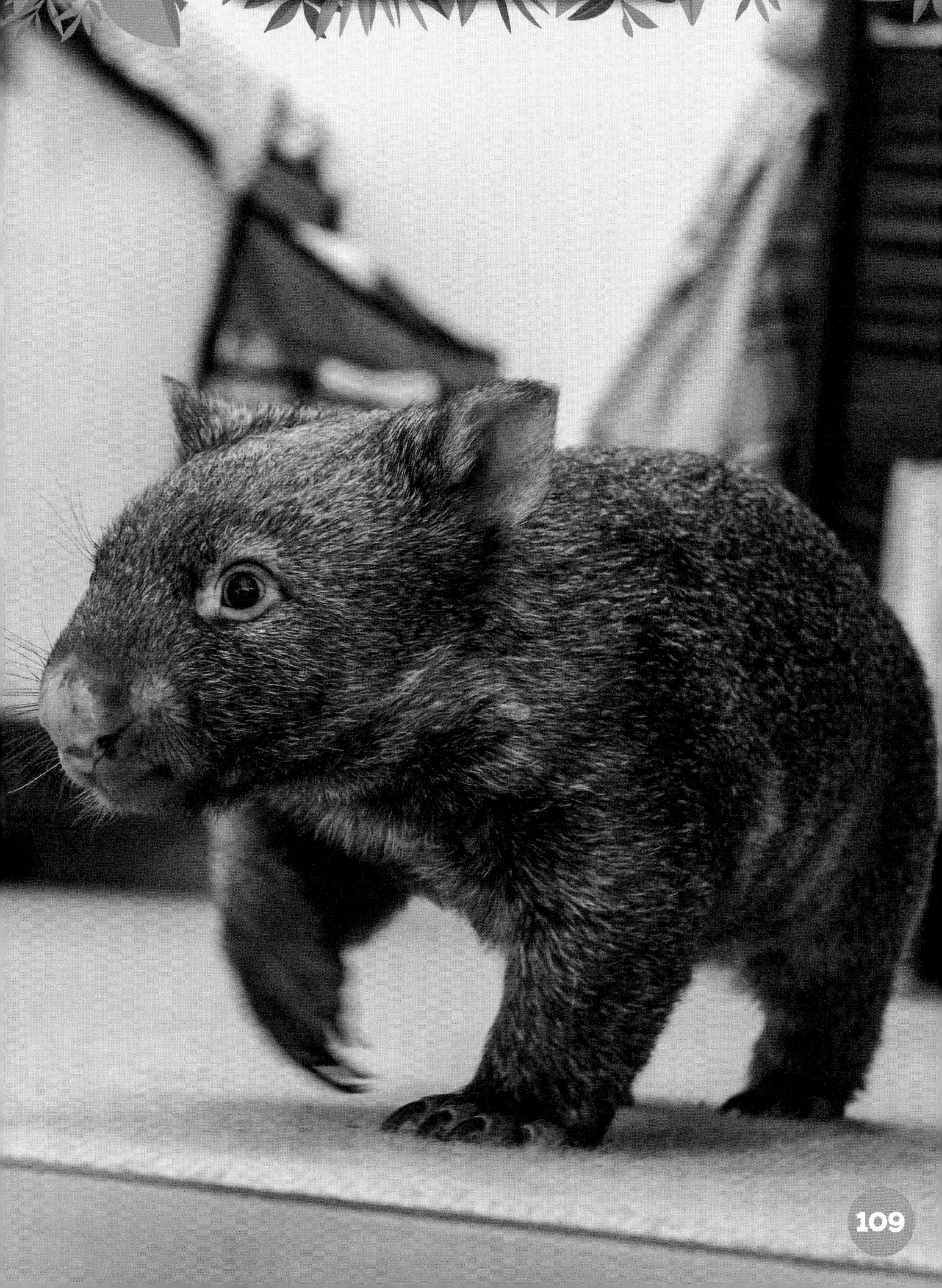

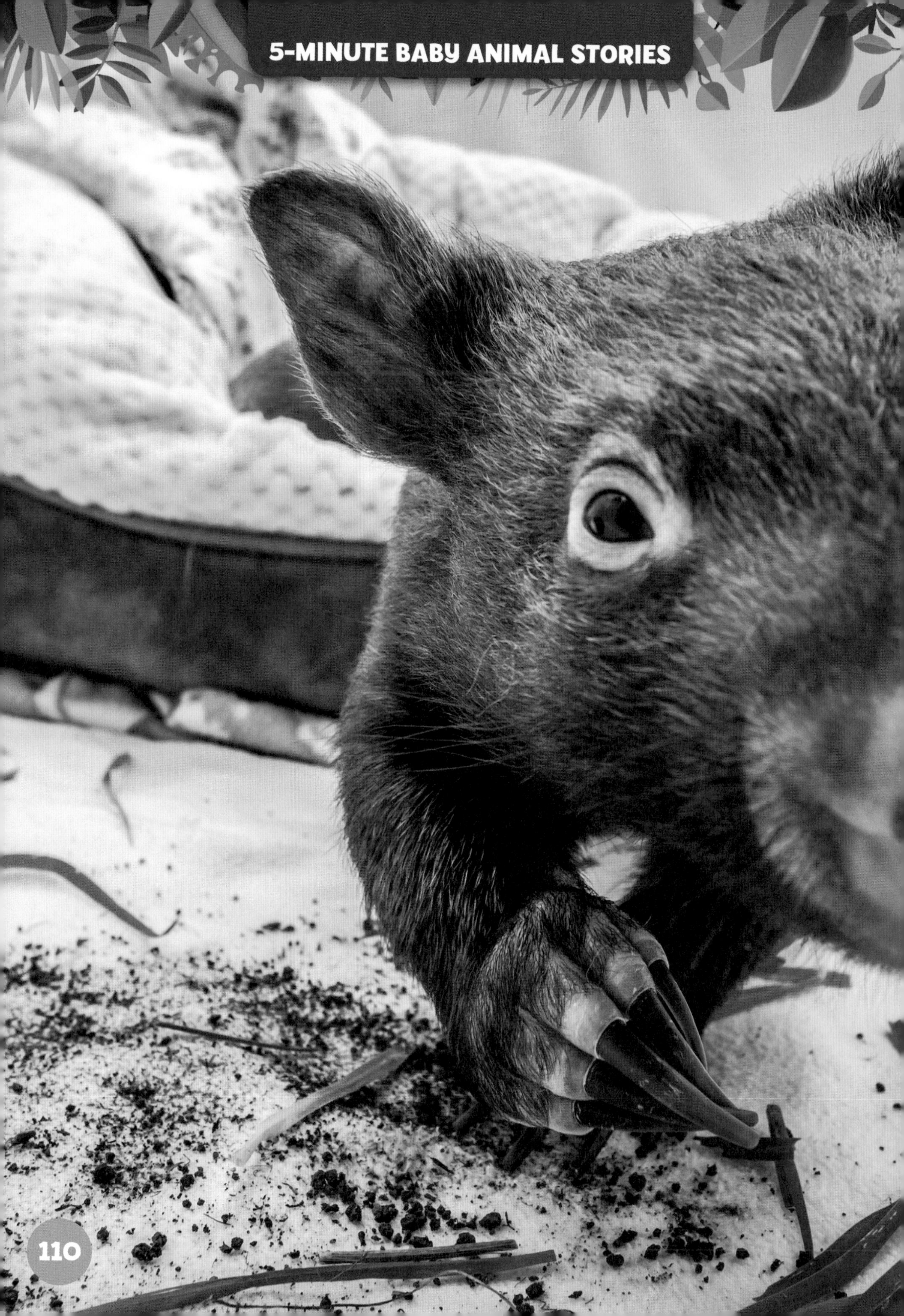

A wombat's
**TEETH NEVER
STOP GROWING.**
They chew on
things to wear
them down.

Wombats like to chew with their beaver-like teeth. Emily gave them sticks to keep them busy. She also gave the joeys grass from the Goongerah area to eat. The babies had to get used to this grass and dirt. It's what they would eat after returning to the wild.

ZZZ

ZZZz

BRONSON AND
LANDON (RIGHT)

For much of the day, the joeys were quiet. They
were still babies, so they spent most of their time
sleeping. Growing takes a lot of energy.

About a month later, another rescued orphan moved in. Her name was Beatrice. Beatrice was a few months older than Bronson and Landon. She was wilder, too. Beatrice quickly became friends with the two male joeys. But she growled at Emily a lot. She didn't trust her human foster mom yet. That stopped once Beatrice learned that Emily would give her food and comfort.

Emily gave the three babies all the health care, milk, and cuddling they needed. But she couldn't give them the kind of company they'd get in the wild. That's why pairing orphan joeys together is so important. It teaches them how to interact with other wombats.

Emily let the joeys do most things they would do in the wild. But she did stop them when they started to dig. In the wild, wombats use their long, super-sharp claws to dig burrows. In Emily's apartment, they just scratched the floor and carpets.

BRONSON AND LANDON (RIGHT)

After three months, Emily took the three wombat joeys back to the wombat orphanage to live in an outdoor enclosure with a ready-made burrow. There they could dig all they wanted!

Orphans usually stay in the orphanage until they are about two years old. Then they are finally released back into the forest where they were born.

WOMBATS spend most of their lives in their BURROWS.

117

Sometimes wombats that grew up in the orphanage find their way back to visit as adults. A few have even brought their own wild-born joeys with them. Emily hopes to one day see Beatrice with a baby of her own! 🐾

From Tiny Tadpoles to Fabulous Frogs

Lots of baby animals

look just like their parents—only smaller. Not frogs! A baby frog doesn't look like an adult frog at all.

That's because frogs go through big changes as they grow up. Their bodies transform from one shape to another. No, it's not magic. This change is called metamorphosis. It is a natural part of the frog's life.

FROG

FROGLET

EGGS

TADPOLE

TADPOLE WITH LEGS

GREEN TREE FROG

121

Frogs start out as tiny eggs. In early spring, just as the weather warms up, the mother frog lays hundreds of round, jellylike eggs. The eggs clump together in a group. The group is called a frogspawn.

COMMON FROG AND FROGSPAWN

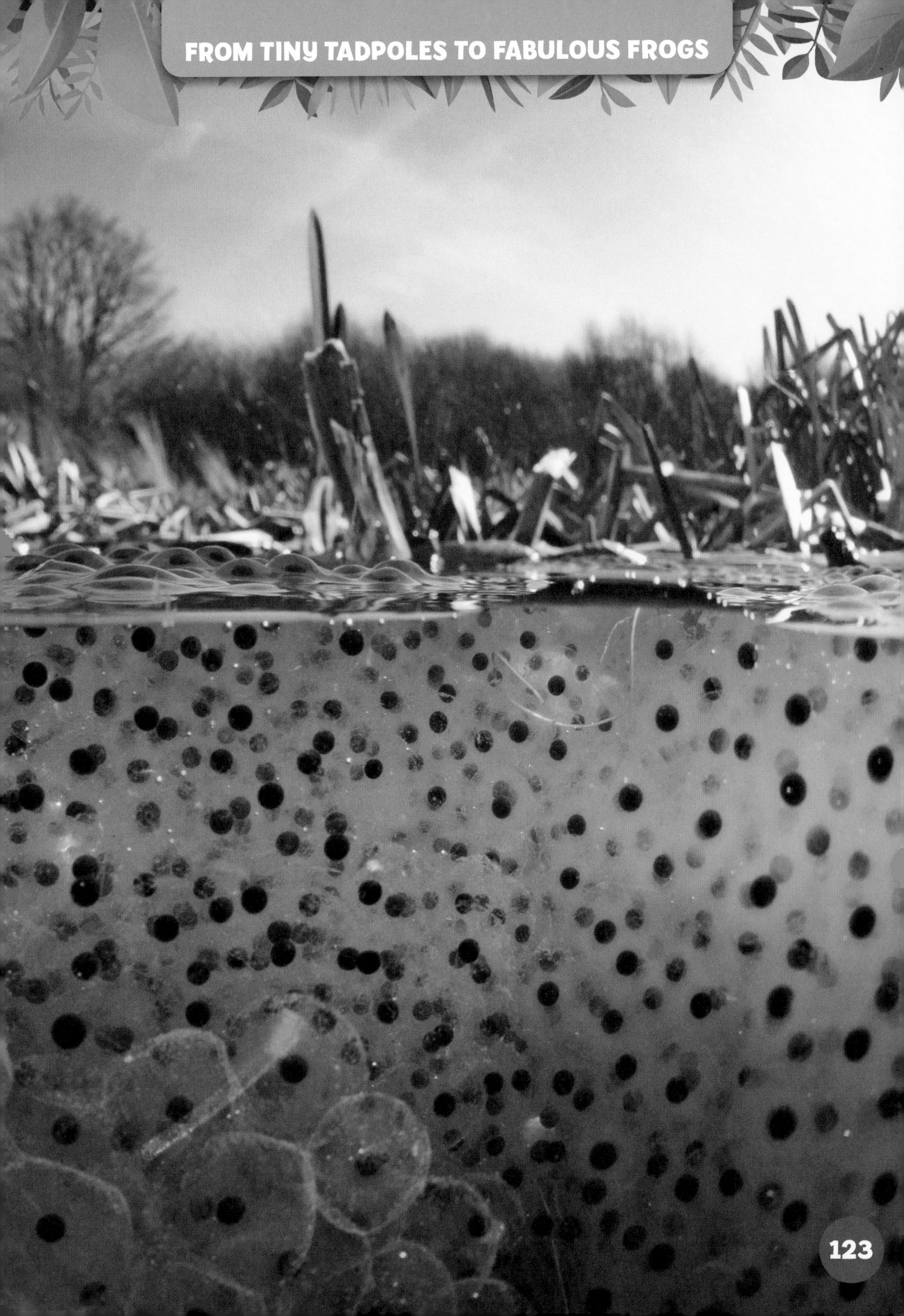

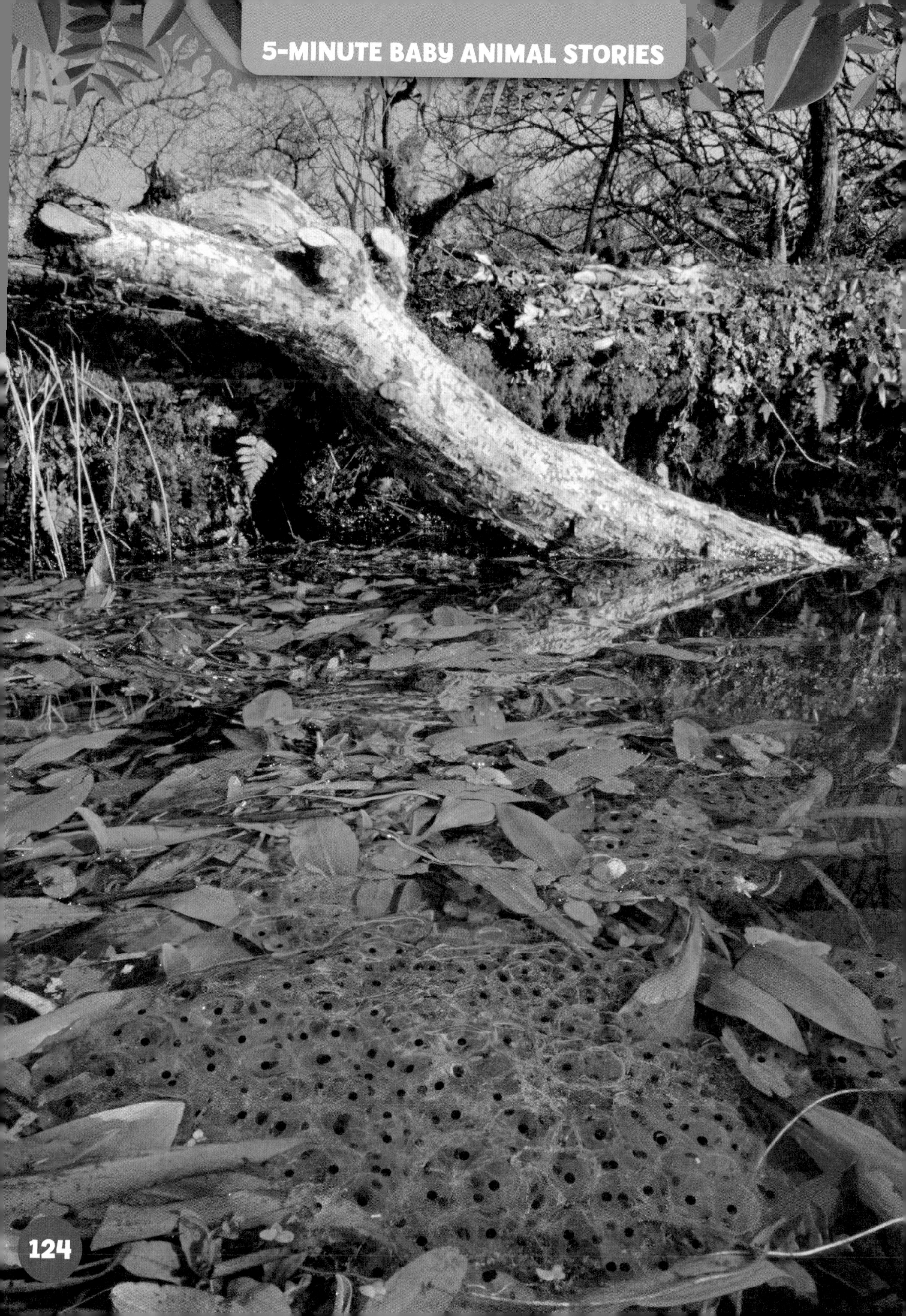

Some mother frogs STAY WITH THEIR EGGS. Others don't.

COMMON FROG

A frogspawn is found in shallow pools of still water, like ponds. The mother frog lays her eggs just below the water's surface. She lays them in a place where they are surrounded by plants. This helps protect the eggs from hungry predators.

If you look closely at the eggs, you can see a tiny black dot in the middle of each one. That's the baby frog! As the days pass, the dot grows. It starts to look like a comma. The baby's tail is starting to grow.

It takes one to three weeks for the eggs to hatch.
The baby frogs that come out are called tadpoles,
or polliwogs.

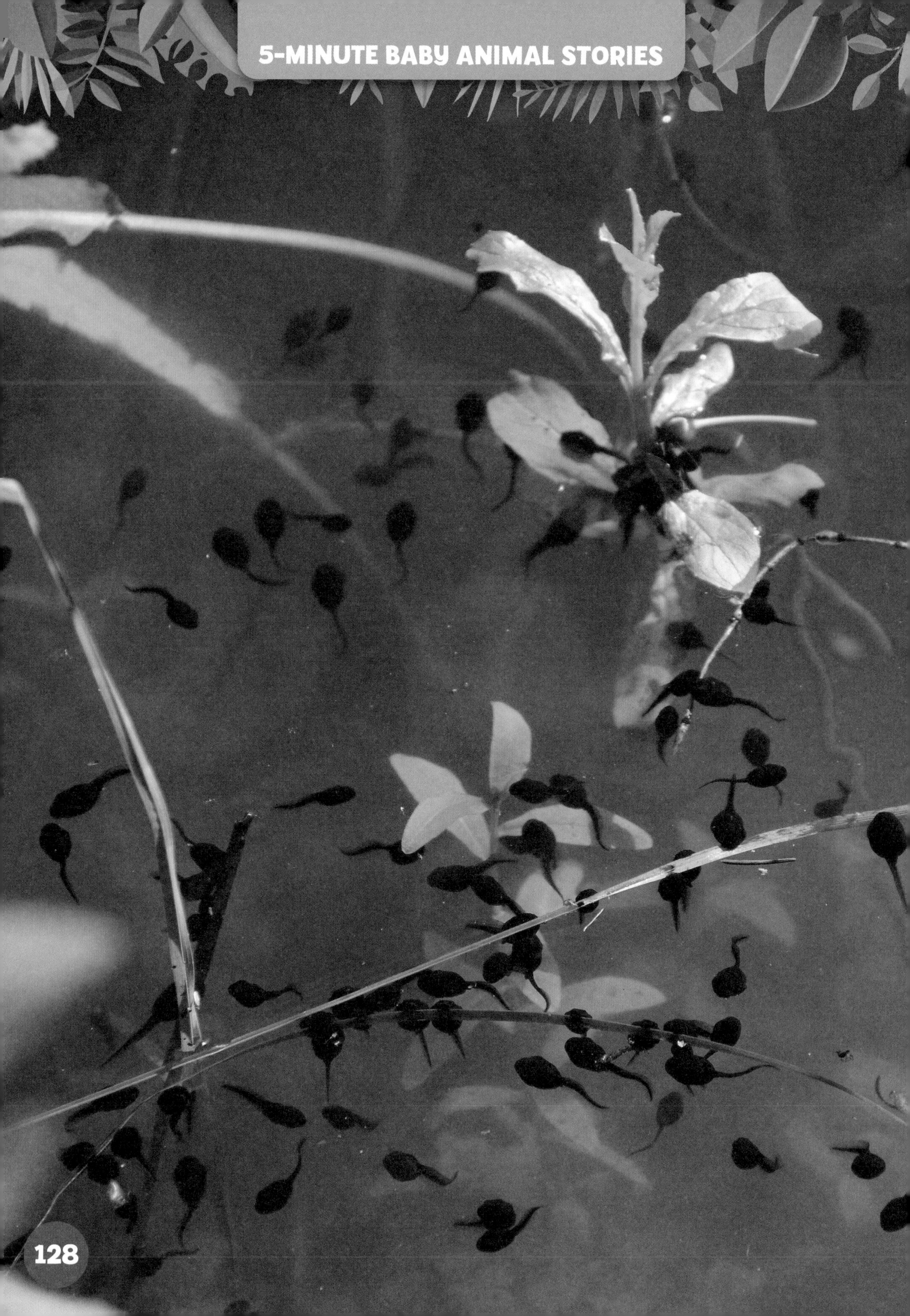

The newborn tadpoles look like little fish with fat heads and long tails. They have gills, which are body parts that help them take oxygen from the water so they can breathe.

For the first few days, the newborn tadpoles rest. They cling to plants in the water.

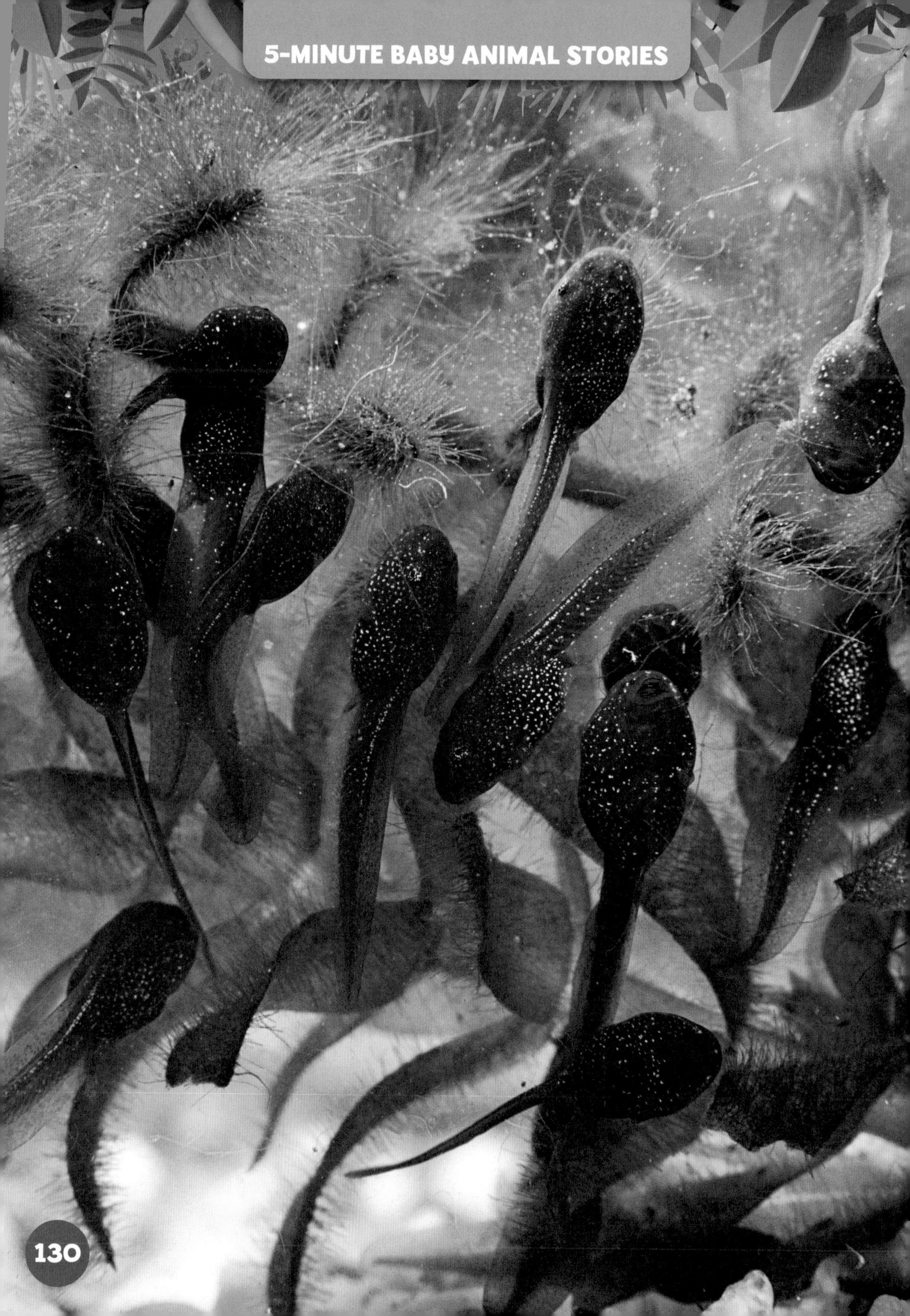

Soon the tadpoles are big and strong enough to explore. They start to eat tiny plants found floating in the water. As they swim and dart, they tear off pieces of plants to eat, too.

A tadpole moves using its TAIL TO SWIM, like a fish!

Finally it is time for metamorphosis to begin! This can happen very quickly or very slowly. It all depends on where the tadpoles live.

When the time is right, the tadpoles' bodies start to go through major changes. First they grow hind legs.

Tadpoles EAT LESS—and GROW MORE SLOWLY—when PREDATORS are around.

Then they grow front legs, too. Their legs get bigger and bigger and bigger.

And then their tails start to shrink, getting smaller and smaller and smaller.

The tadpoles' bodies are changing inside, too. They develop lungs. Skin grows over their gills. But that's not a problem because they don't need to breathe in the water anymore. Now they can breathe on land!

WOOD FROG
FROGLET

The tadpole is not a tadpole anymore. It is a froglet, or a tiny adult. And it's ready to make its grand entrance on land!

FROGLETS don't eat much. They get nutrients when they ABSORB THEIR TAILS!

Many frogs can jump more than 20 TIMES THEIR BODY LENGTH!

TREE FROG

The froglet hops out of the pond. It jumps across the land. It begins eating insects, small spiders, and worms. Soon it will grow bigger and become a fully grown frog. It will hop, hop, hop to a pond to lay eggs, and the cycle will start all over again! 🐾

Jaguar Cub Cuties

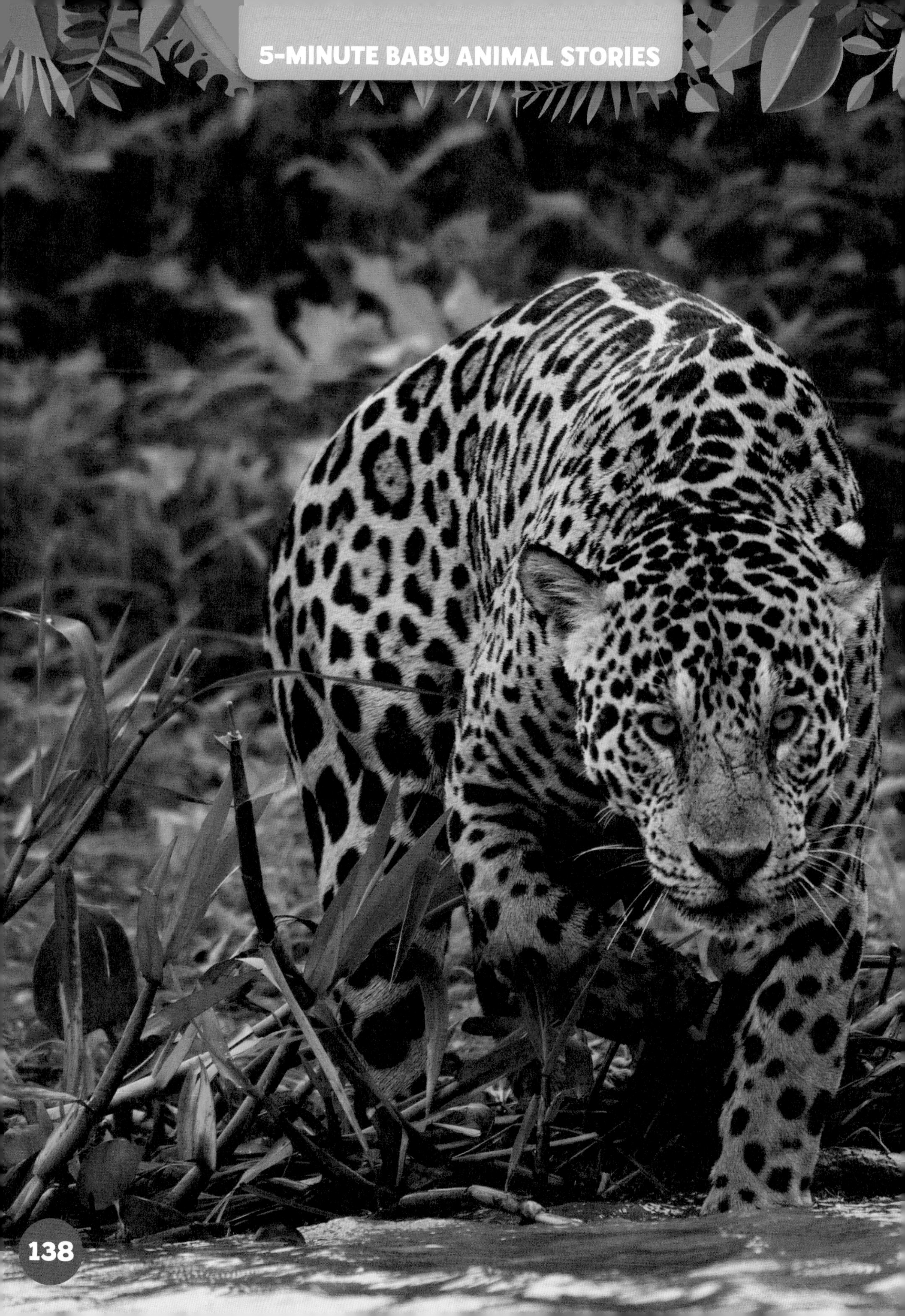

A female jaguar walks through the rainforest. She sees a cave on the riverbank and walks in to take a look. The cave is nearly hidden among rocks. Thick plants cover its opening. This cave will make a good den. It will be a good place to have her cubs.

When the jaguar's cubs are born, they are deaf, blind, and toothless. Each one weighs less than two pounds (1 kg). That's about the weight of a pineapple.

Like their mother, the cubs have yellow-orange fur covered with black spots. These spots are called rosettes. But some jaguars are born with black fur. You have to look closely to see that they have rosettes in their fur, too.

Taking care of the cubs is a full-time job for the mother. She raises them on her own. All other jaguars are a threat. If necessary, the mother will fight them to keep her babies safe.

The helpless cubs grow fast. Within two weeks, their eyes open so they can see. Within a month, they have teeth. Now, in addition to drinking their mother's milk, they can also eat meat that she brings into the den. Yum!

As the cubs grow, the den becomes a noisy, busy place. The cubs jump and play. They cough and grunt! They bark and roar! And of course they meow!

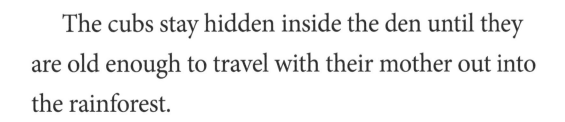

The cubs stay hidden inside the den until they are old enough to travel with their mother out into the rainforest.

When the cubs are ready, the mother jaguar waits until night and leads them out of the den. The cautious cubs explore. They sniff the ground and investigate rocks and bushes. They climb slippery slopes with their sharp claws as they make their way through the rainforest.

Jaguars LIVE ALONE, except when mothers are raising their babies.

The nightly lessons begin. The mother jaguar teaches the cubs how to climb a tree. Then she teaches them how to hunt like she does. Jaguars don't chase their prey like other big cats do. They go out at night and sit silently in a tree. When an unlucky deer or capybara walks below, they pounce!

Most cats don't like water, but it doesn't bother jaguars. The mother jaguar takes her cubs to the river and leads them across. The cubs learn how to swim.

Jaguars have been known to SWIM ACROSS THE PANAMA CANAL!

JAGUAR AND CAIMAN

The mother jaguar shows the cubs how to grab prey like turtles and caimans with their sharp teeth. She also shows them how to fish. They tap their tails on the water's surface. When curious fish respond, the cubs grab them with their claws. What a tasty meal!

149

As the cubs travel through the rainforest, their mother shows them different ways to mark their territory. They scrape the ground with their hind paws. They claw and scratch the trees. They rub their heads on things to leave their scent.

Sometimes they leave a smellier scent—pee and poo. When other animals get a whiff, they know whose territory they are in.

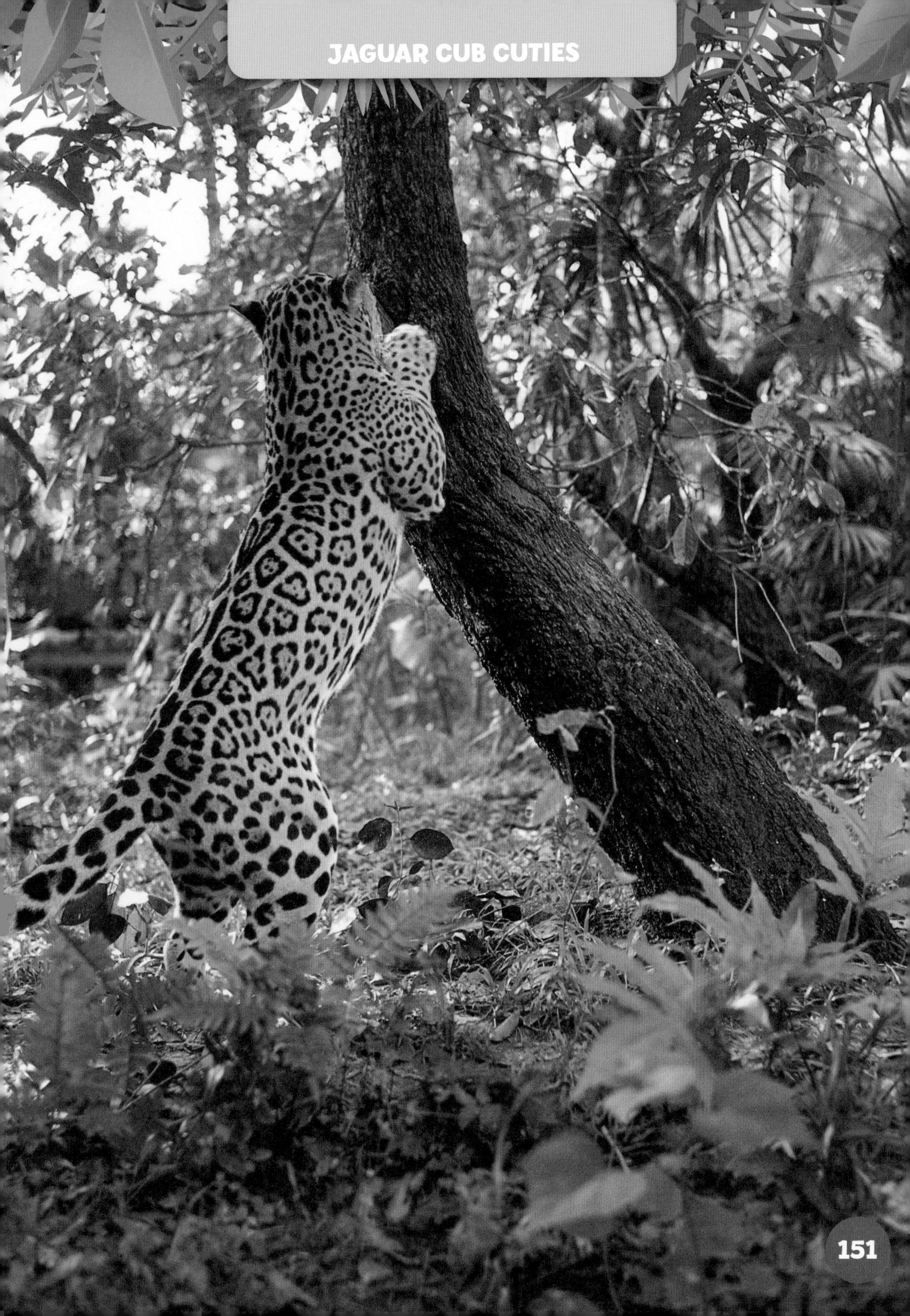

When the cubs are a year old, they start hunting on their own. The cubs leave their mother and wander through her territory in the rainforest.

But the cubs always return to the den. They're not ready to leave their mother quite yet. They still need her protection.

Jaguars have the STRONGEST JAWS of all cat species.

Another year passes. At around two years old, the cubs have learned all the skills they need to survive on their own. One by one, the cubs leave their mother.

Full-grown and independent at last, they venture out into the rainforest to find territories of their own. 🐾

Manatee Man to the Rescue

National Geographic

Explorer Jamal Galves was at home watching a movie with his family in Belize when the phone rang. Someone had seen a baby manatee. For two days, it had been swimming all alone in an abandoned marine fish farm. This was not good news. Baby manatees, called calves, need their mothers.

Why call Jamal? He's the Manatee Man! Ever since he was a kid, he has wanted to know more about these gentle giants. He loved manatees so much that his friends started calling him Manatee Man, and the name stuck. Now he spends his time trying to save this endangered species.

Jamal gathered the members of his marine rescue team. It would take about 45 minutes to get to the fish farm, and they needed to get there as quickly as they could.

Baby manatees are curious little creatures. They don't stay in one place very long.

MANATEES are related to ELEPHANTS!

159

Luckily, when they arrived they spotted the calf right away. It was swimming in circles and breathing very rapidly. It was stressed out and needed help. But first they had to make sure the baby really was alone. They flew a drone over the fish farm to search for its mother. She was not there.

Jamal walked slowly into the warm water, inching his way toward the baby. The baby manatee saw him and quickly swam away. It was scared of Jamal, so he stopped moving. Slowly, the calf calmed down and swam closer to him—but not close enough for him to safely grab it.

Then the curious baby started to swim in circles around Jamal. It was starting to understand that he was not a threat. Each time the manatee put its head underwater, Jamal moved a little closer to it.

Finally, he was close enough. Quickly but gently, Jamal wrapped his arms around the little manatee. At first, the calf wiggled. But once Jamal held the baby securely against his body, it relaxed.

A **NEWBORN** manatee weighs at least **60 POUNDS** (27 kg)!

Jamal carried the baby out of the water and handed it to a member of his team. He laid it on a layer of soft foam in the back of their rescue truck. They examined the calf. He was a boy. He had some small scratches, but no major injuries.

The baby manatee was very thin, though, and needed liquids. Manatees don't have much body fat to keep them warm, and they need to stay wet. So the rescuers wrapped the baby in a towel and sprayed the towel with water. Then they fed him with a bottle and headed for the rescue center.

It was a long journey. The Wildtracks rehab center is located in a small village in northern Belize. It was four hours away from the fish farm. The calf stayed calm and hungrily drank from the bottle they gave him every hour during the trip.

MANATEE MAN TO THE RESCUE

167

Once they arrived, Jamal carried the baby into the rehab center. He placed him in a pool of water that the workers had prepared. The tired little manatee seemed eager to be in the water again. The rescuers' job was done. Now it was up to the staff and volunteers at the rehab center to help the baby manatee become strong and healthy.

The people at the rehab center named the calf Teek. For the first few days, they watched Teek constantly. Manatees live in water, but they are mammals and need to swim to the surface to breathe air. The volunteers observed Teek to make sure his breathing was OK.

When RESTING, a manatee can STAY UNDERWATER for up to 20 MINUTES.

169

Manatees constantly grow
NEW TEETH
that replace the
old ones.

Every two hours, someone fed Teek a bottle of milk. He was also given bottles of a special drink to prevent dehydration. Teek was only three or four weeks old. He didn't have any teeth yet. In the wild, he would have drunk his mother's milk until he was old enough to eat solid food.

Teek's journey to recovery will be long. The rehab team will teach him what manatee mothers teach their babies in the wild so they can survive.

Once Teek is ready, the team will release him back into the waters where other manatees live. He will join a big group, called a herd. The manatees in the herd will become his new family. Until then, Teek will continue to grow bigger and stronger at the rehab center. The people there are his family now. 🐾

A Panda Cub Grows Up

A giant panda lives in a bamboo forest high in the mountains of south-central China. The forests are cool and wet. Most of the time she lives alone, munching on bamboo—her favorite food.

FEMALE giant pandas have their first **BABIES** when they are **BETWEEN FOUR AND SIX YEARS OLD.**

A **DEN** is a place where **WILD ANIMALS REST** or **FIND SHELTER.**

But in the spring, the female panda is going to have a baby. She searches for a hollow tree to use as a den. She needs a safe place to give birth.

The panda makes a nest out of branches and grass. The nest is tiny. But that's OK, because her baby will be tiny, too. It's about the size of a stick of butter!

After the cub is born, it snuggles in its mother's warm arms. Its eyes are closed, so it cannot see. Fine white hairs are sprinkled across its wrinkly pink body.

The toothless cub spends all of its time sleeping or drinking its mother's milk. It croaks and squeals loudly when it is hungry. The baby is helpless. But don't worry. The mother panda will take good care of her cub.

The baby's body changes quickly. Black patches appear on its skin. Black fur grows in the patches. In a few weeks, the cub looks like a miniature adult. Its teeth even start to come in.

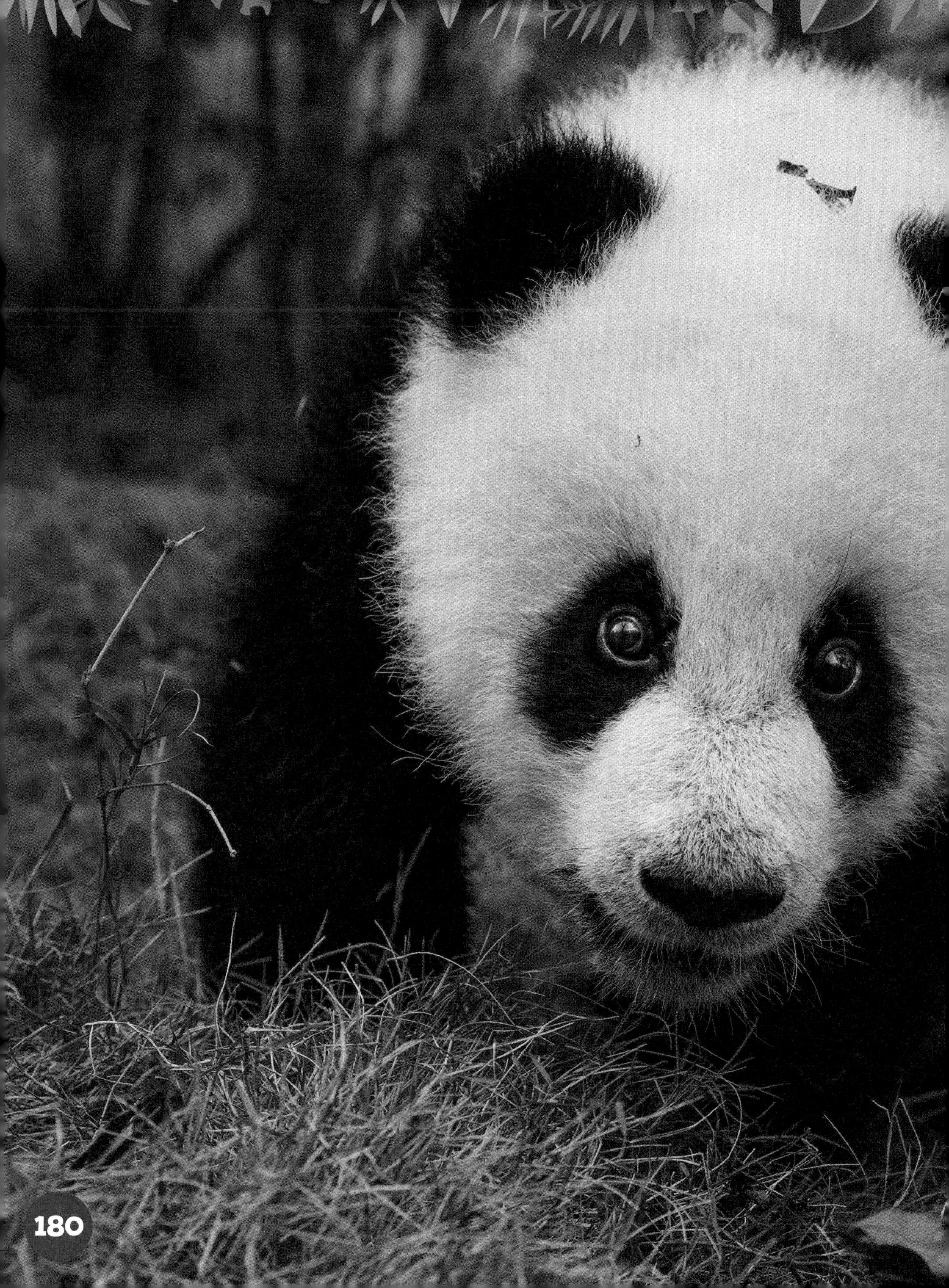

Panda cubs **START TO WALK** when they are about **THREE MONTHS OLD.**

As the baby grows, it starts to move around the den. At first, the cub crawls and scoots along the ground. Then it stands on all four legs. Finally, it starts to walk. It's a wobbly walk, but it works!

The cub is now a clumsy, fluffy ball of black and white fur. It tumbles and rolls on the ground. It plays with its mother, climbs on her back, and follows her

The two pandas sit in the treetops for hours—or even days—at a time. The mother panda knows this is a good place to keep the cub safe from predators.

Now that the cub can explore, the mother starts teaching some important lessons. Lesson number one is how to find bamboo. Pandas spend up to 16 hours a day looking for and eating food. Most of that food is bamboo. The mother panda shows the cub where to find bamboo in the forest.

Finding bamboo is one thing. Eating it is another. The cub watches its mother. It holds the stalk in its front paws and plucks off the leaves. The cub's mother crushes and chews the stalk with her flat back teeth. The cub will need practice to do that. It's a good thing the cub is still drinking its mother's milk.

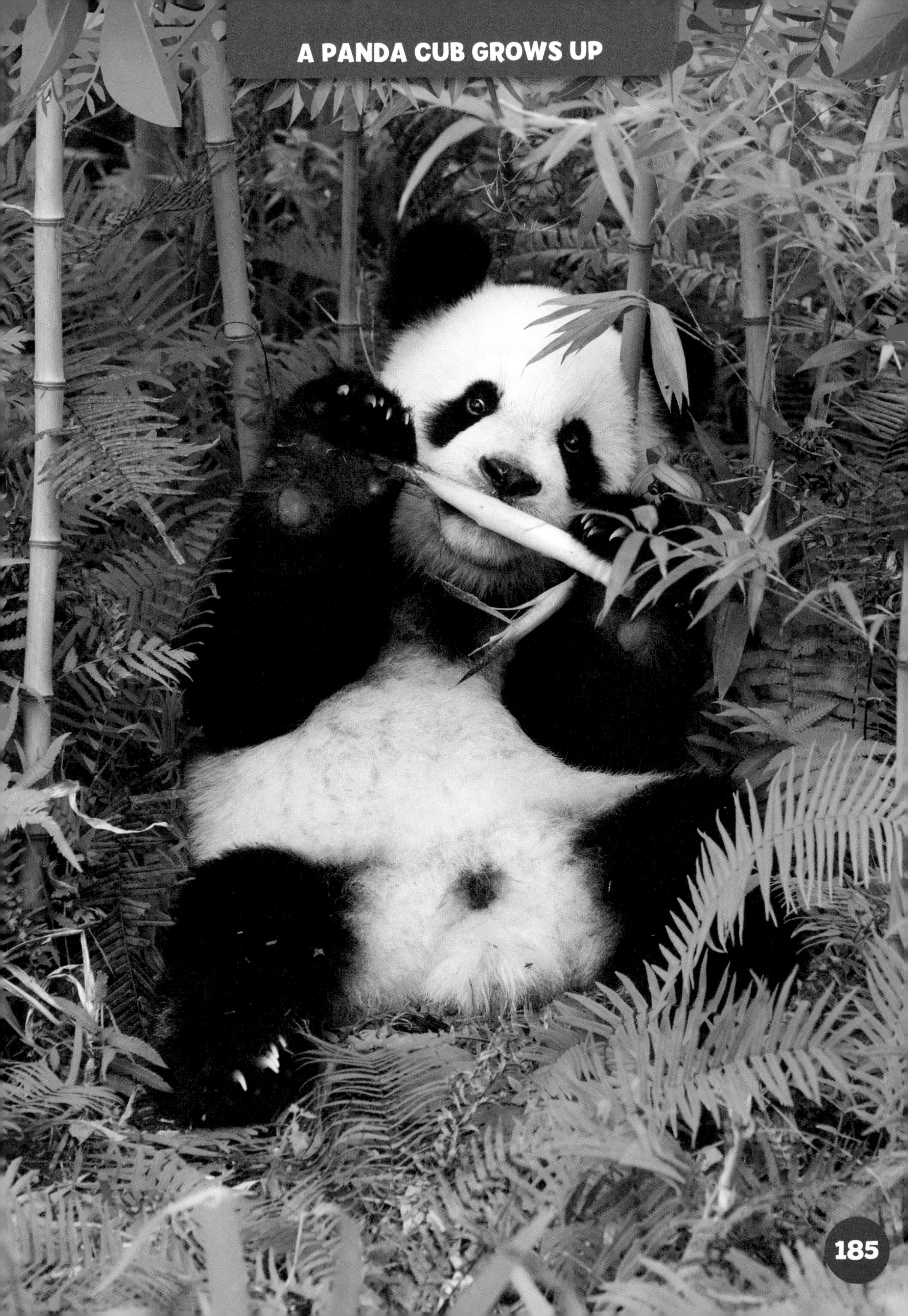

As a newborn, the cub croaked and squealed. Now it honks, huffs, barks, and growls just like its mother. That is how they communicate.

Baby pandas can do SOMERSAULTS. They also like to SLIDE IN THE SNOW.

The mother panda also teaches the baby how to communicate with other pandas and mark its territory. She shows the cub how to leave its scent behind. The baby lifts its tail and squirts a waxy substance on trees, rocks, bamboo, and bushes. It might even do a handstand to make the mark higher on a tree.

PANDAS spend almost all their time EATING and SLEEPING.

After one year, the panda cub is 60 pounds (27 kg) of roly-poly fun. It has all of its adult teeth and can munch on a meal of bamboo. But the young panda will drink its mother's milk for six more months. So it sticks close to its mother's side.

The cub continues to grow. Once it is big enough, the cub stays by itself when the mother panda goes out to find food. The cub spends hours alone, sleeping in the treetops until its mother returns.

By the time the cub is three years old, it has learned all it can from its mother. It knows how to find and eat bamboo. It knows how to communicate with other pandas. It knows how to find and protect its territory. The cub is all grown up!

That means it's time for the grown-up cub to live on its own. Using the lessons learned when it was a baby, the panda will find its own way through the forest. The mother panda has taught it well. 🐾

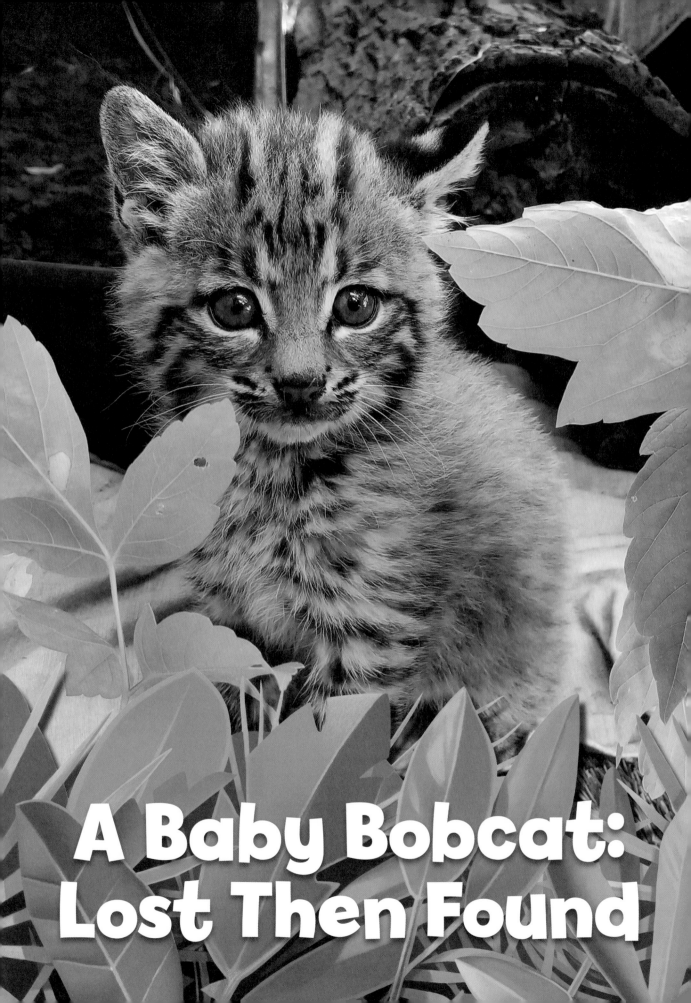

A Baby Bobcat: Lost Then Found

Bobcats are the **MOST COMMON WILD CAT** in North America.

One summer, a tiny kitten wobbled up the Drown Road Trail in Marin County, California, U.S.A. The kitten followed a pair of hikers up the path. The hikers didn't see her. But someone else did. He wondered why a cat was on the hiking trail.

The man got closer. He saw spots on the little cat's fur. This was no ordinary house cat. It was a wild bobcat kitten! It had lost its mother. It was in trouble! The man wrapped the frightened kitten inside a sweatshirt. He took it to a nearby ranger station.

The park ranger was surprised. Bobcats are shy animals. People rarely see their kittens. The ranger called the local Humane Society. They took the kitten to WildCare, a place that takes care of sick, injured, or orphaned wild animals.

Melanie and Jacqueline were working at WildCare. They were surprised to see a bobcat kitten, too. In her 15 years at WildCare, Melanie had never received a bobcat kitten!

Bobcat kittens STAY WITH THEIR MOTHER for about a year.

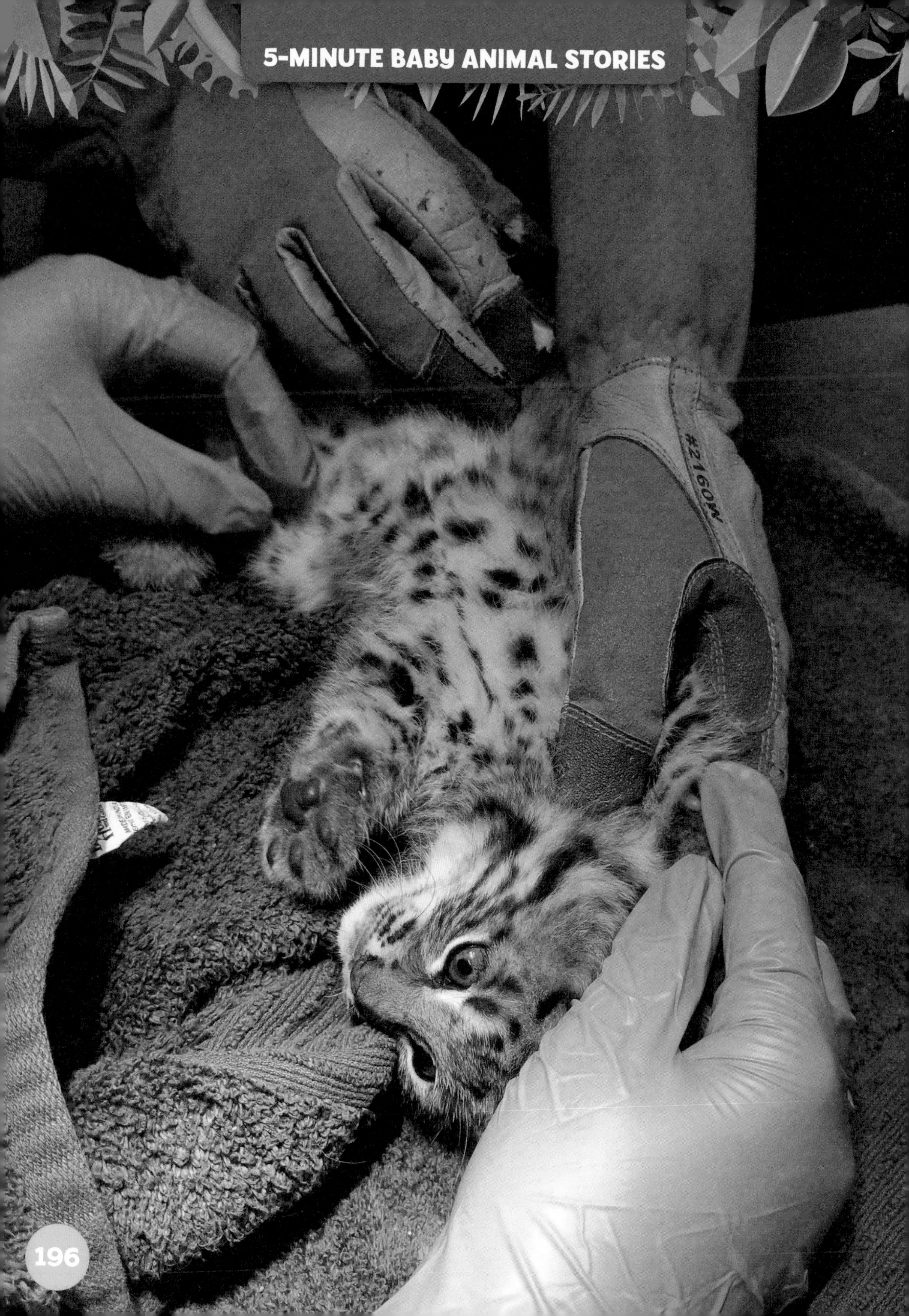
#2160W

Melanie and Jacqueline examined the kitten. She weighed only 1.2 pounds (554 g). She was covered in ticks, and she was dehydrated and needed liquids. Melanie gave the kitten a shot of fluids and medicine for ticks and fleas.

The baby bobcat needed a quiet place to rest, so she was placed in a wire-framed kennel away from the main building and people. She was given a pink stuffed cat for company.

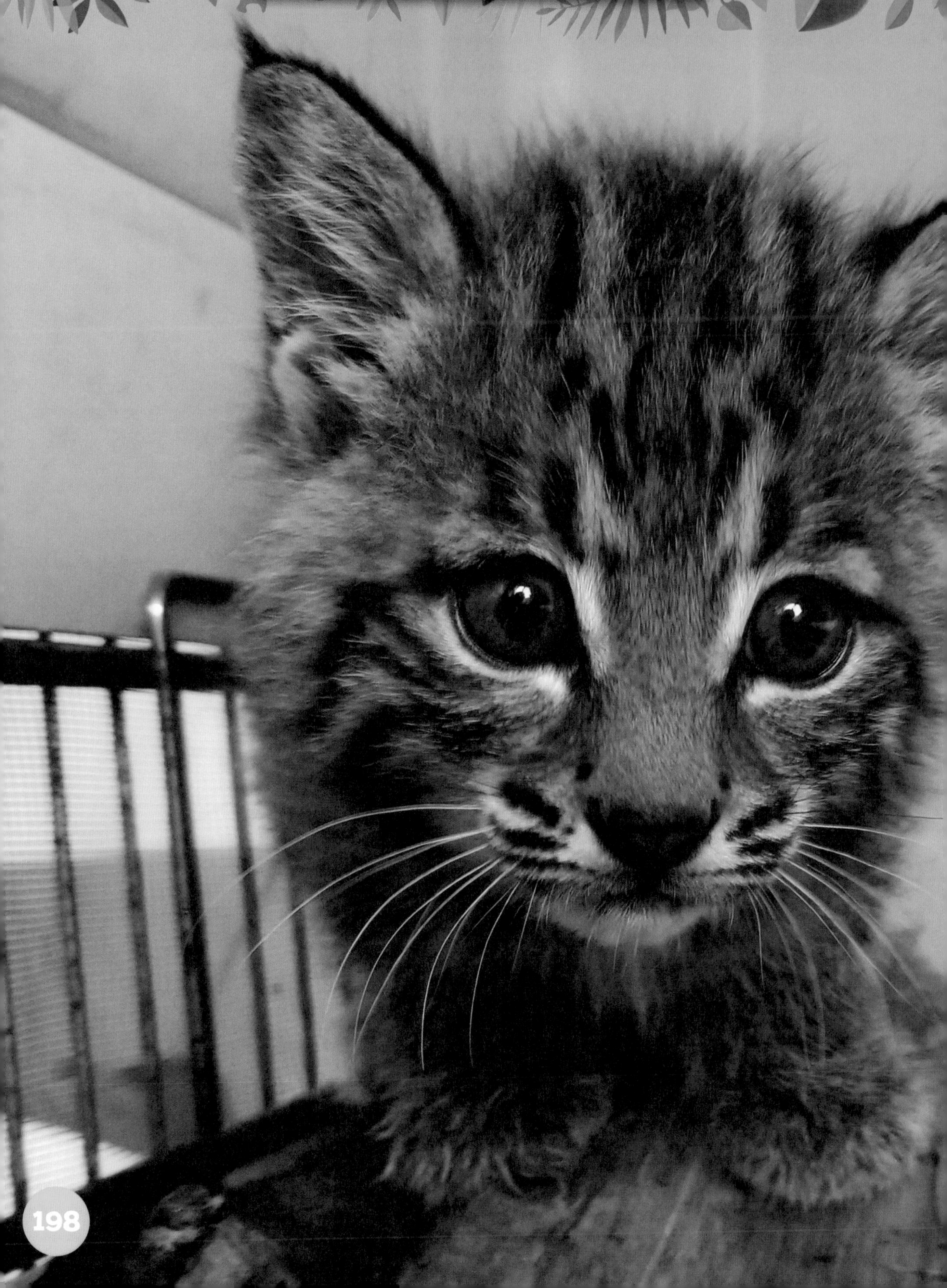

Melanie became the kitten's main caretaker. She hid a video camera inside the kennel so she could watch the kitten from her office. To keep from getting too attached to her, she called the kitten by her patient ID number—1874—instead of giving her a name.

This care was only a temporary solution. The kitten needed to grow up with other young bobcats. That is how she would learn to hunt, fight, play, and live like a wild bobcat. WildCare found the perfect place. Sierra Wildlife Rescue had two bobcat kittens, and it was only two hours away!

Bobcats are named for their short, or "BOBBED," TAIL.

Kitten 1874 was in WildCare's hospital, giving her time to become healthy and strong. Then a volunteer drove 1874 to her next home. Jill, a Sierra Wildlife volunteer, let the kitten rest for a few hours. Then she examined the new arrival. The tiny bobcat weighed just under two pounds (907 g). She was bright-eyed and healthy. 1874 would be at the center for at least six months, so Jill gave her a name. From now on, the little bobcat would be called Ember.

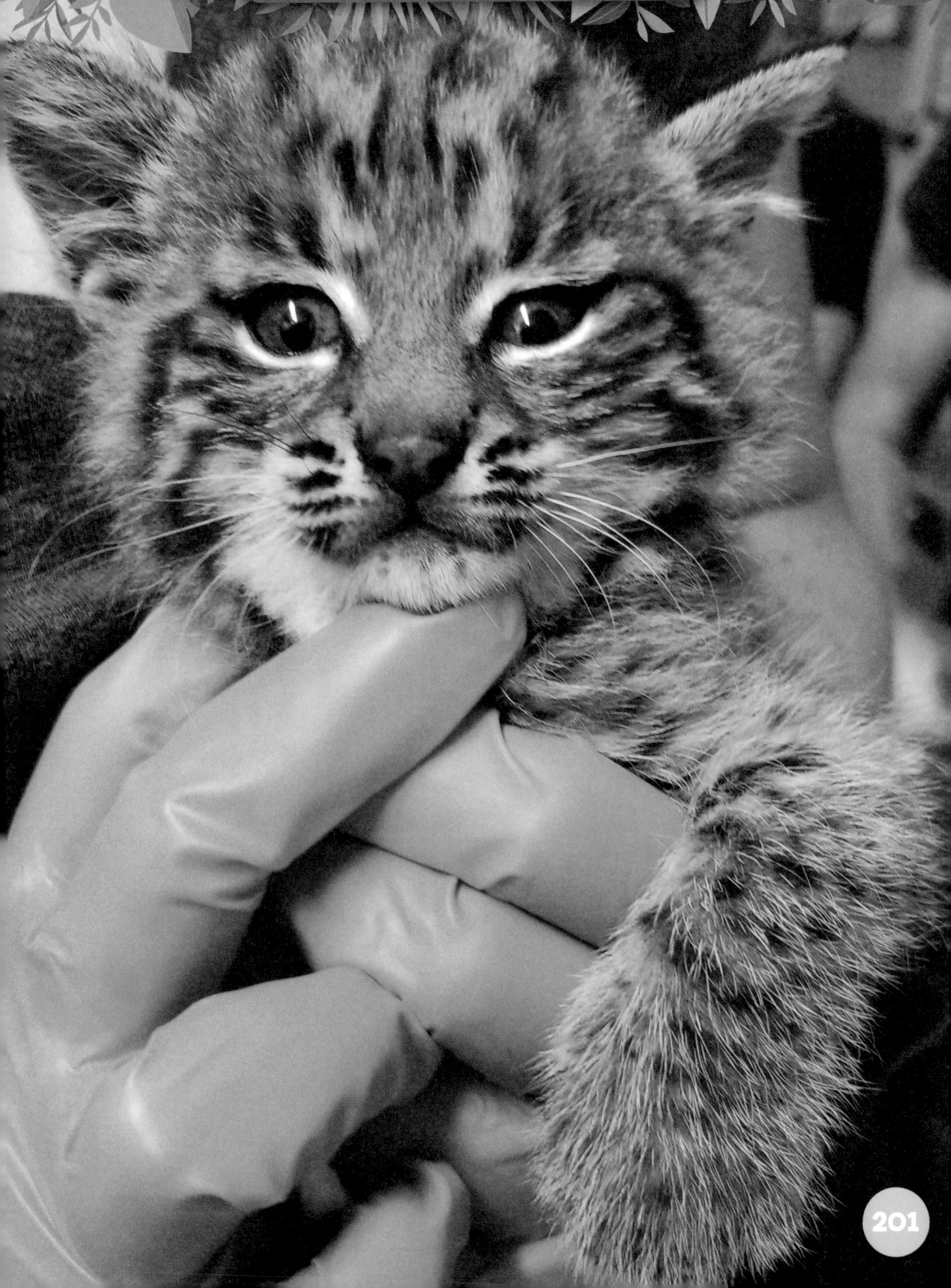

Ember moved into a new kennel. The kennel had shelves for sleeping and things to play with. Best of all, it was quiet.

Soon, it was time to meet the other young bobcats, Evan and Elsa. Jill rolled Ember's kennel into their enclosure. Before letting Ember out, she gave the bobcats time to get used to each other.

EMBER (LEFT), EVAN, AND ELSA (RIGHT)

Adult bobcats LIVE ALONE. Each one has ITS OWN TERRITORY.

Inside her kennel, Ember looked down as Evan stretched up, trying to get closer. Elsa jumped on the roof of Ember's kennel. She leaned down to peek inside. Ember stared at them with curious eyes.

203

One week later, Jill opened Ember's door. The three kittens tumbled over one another, rolling and playing. This was going to work! Ember had a new home with new friends.

Over the next few months, Ember enjoyed her new home. Regular visits to the veterinarian ensured that she was healthy and growing. Soon she was up to seven pounds (3 kg)!

A FULL-GROWN BOBCAT is TWO to THREE TIMES BIGGER than a HOUSE CAT.

EVAN (TOP) AND ELSA

In October, Ember, Elsa, and Evan got a new room-mate, a female bobcat named Echo. The four young bobcats climbed and pounced and slept in a heap.

By November, Ember was old enough, and had learned all the skills needed, to be released back into the wild. But it was too late in the fall. Food would be harder to find, and wildfires had damaged the area where Ember was born. She would stay at Sierra Wildlife with the other young bobcats until the following spring.

EMBER AND EVAN (RIGHT)

206

Finally it was time for one last car trip. Ember was driven near where she was found on Drown Road Trail. Her carrier door was opened, and she slipped into the woods without looking back. Ember wasn't a frightened kitten anymore. She was safe, and she was home.

Published by National Geographic Partners, LLC, Washington, DC 20036.

Designed by Brett Challos

Library of Congress Cataloging-in-Publication Data

Names: National Geographic Kids (Firm), publisher.
Title: National Geographic Kids 5-minute baby animal stories.
Description: Washington, D.C. : National Geographic Kids, [2023]
Identifiers: LCCN 2021061171 | ISBN 9781426374791 (hardcover)
Subjects: LCSH: Animals--Infancy--Juvenile literature.
Classification: LCC QL763 .N38 2023 | DDC 591.3/92--dc23/
   eng/20211222
LC record available at https://lccn.loc.gov/2021061171

ACKNOWLEDGMENTS

The publisher would like to thank National Geographic Explorer Jamal Galves for sharing his story for this book. The publisher also thanks the following organizations: Clearwater Marine Aquarium Research Institute (cmaresearchinstitute.org); International Animal Rescue (internationalanimalrescue.org); Wolves Offered Life and Friendship (wolfsanctuary.co); Sheldrick Wildlife Trust (sheldrickwildlifetrust.org); Kenya Wildlife Service (kws.go.ke); Goongerah Wombat Orphanage (goongerahwombatorphanage.org); Wildtracks (wildtracksusa.org); WildCare (discoverwildcare.org); Sierra Wildlife Rescue (sierrawildliferescue.org); Marin County Humane Society (marinhumane.org); Big Bones Canine Rescue (bigbonescaninerescue.com); Veterinary Teaching Hospital at Colorado State University (vetmedbiosci.colostate.edu/vth/).

Thanks also to Libby Romero, writer; Michelle Harris, fact-checker; Angela Modany and Lisa M. Gerry, editors; Lori Epstein, photo director; Brett Challos, designer; Alix Inchausti, senior production editor; and Anne LeongSon and Gus Tello, associate designers.

PHOTO CREDITS

AD=Adobe Stock; AL=Alamy Stock Photo; GI=Getty Images; MP=Minden Pictures; NGIC=National Geographic Image Collection; NPL=Nature Picture Library; SS=Shutterstock

Front Cover: (leaves), Robert Hynes and Jeffrey Mangiat/Mendola LTD; (bamboo), Dualororua/SS; (panda), Eric Baccega/NPL; (owl), Jim Cumming/AD; (jaguar), ZSSD/MP; (frog), kuritafsheen/AD; **Spine:** Ana Gram/SS; **Back Cover:** (turtle), Roger Le Guen/ Biosphoto; (background), Ana Gram/SS; **Interior:** header artwork, Robert Hynes and Jeffrey Mangiat/Mendola LTD; 1 (background), Ana Gram/SS; 1 (leaves), Robert Hynes and Jeffrey Mangiat/Mendola LTD; 1 (frog), kuritafsheen/AD; **Learning at the Ape Academy:** 3-7, International Animal Rescue/Future Publishing/GI; 8-18, International Animal Rescue; **A Baby Sea Turtle's Journey:** 19, Joel Sartore/NGIC; 20-21, Brian J. Skerry/NGIC; 22-23, Doug Perrine/ Blue Planet Archive; 24, Heinrich van den Berg/AL; 25, Beachmite Photography/GI; 26, Jurgen Freund/NPL; 27, Roger Le Guen/ Biosphoto; 28, Thomas P. Peschak/NGIC; 29, Brian J. Skerry/NGIC; 30-31, Jurgen Freund/NPL; 32-33, Herve06/GI; 34-35, Paulo de Oliveira/Biosphoto; 36, Brian J. Skerry/NGIC; **Ashima the Wolf Dog:** 37-52, W.O.L.F. Sanctuary; **Supercool Penguin Chicks:** 53, Jan Vermeer/MP; 54-55, Samuel Blanc/Biosphoto; 56, David Tipling/ Biosphoto; 57-60, Stefan Christmann/NPL; 61, Samuel Blanc/ Biosphoto; 62, BIA/Stefan Christmann/Biosphoto; 63, Doug Allan/ NPL; 64-65, Tui De Roy/MP; 66-67, Fred Olivier/NPL; 68, Stefan Christmann/NPL; **A Home for Baby Elephants:** 69, Robert Henno/ AL; 70, Inaki Relanzon/NPL; 71, Suzi Eszterhas/MP; 72, THE DSWT/Future Publishing/GI; 73, Jason Edwards/NGIC; 74, Michael Nichols/NGIC; 75, Lisa Hoffner/NPL; 76, Michael Nichols/NGIC; 77, The David Sheldrick Wildlife Trust; 78-79, Lisa Hoffner/NPL; 80, Jason Edwards/NGIC; 81, The David Sheldrick Wildlife Trust; 82-83, 84, Lisa Hoffner/NPL; **Hoot, Hoot, Hooray!:** 85, jimcumming88/ AD; 86, Bengt Lundberg/NPL; 87, NPL/AL; 88, imageBROKER/AL; 89, Denise Iacangelo/SS; 90, FLPA/MP; 91, blickwinkel/AL; 92, Donald M. Jones/MP; 93, Tom Vezo/MP; 94, Rob Reijnen/NiS/MP; 95, Jack Dykinga/NPL; 96, Jillian/AD; 97, Ernst Dirksen/Buiten-beeld/MP; 98, Xavier Eichaker/Biosphoto; 99, Jack Dykinga/NPL; 100, Adri Hoogendijk/NiS/MP; **Wombat Rescue!:** 101, Doug Gimesy/NPL; 102, Alba Boix/AL; 103, Ian Lumsden/GI; 104-115, Doug Gimesy/NPL; 116-117, mauritius images GmbH/AL; 118, Doug Gimesy/NPL; **From Tiny Tadpoles to Fabulous Frogs:** 119, kuritafsheen/AD; 120-121, Agus/AD; 120 (inset), Kazakova Maryia/AD; 122-123, David Tipling/NPL; 124, Nick Upton/NPL; 125, Bernard Castelein/NPL; 126, Stephen Dalton/NPL; 127, ELKOKREATIV/AD; 128-129, Claudia Evans/AD; 130, Jane Burton/ NPL; 131, Willem Kolvoort/NPL; 132, 133, Fabio Liverani/NPL; 134-135, Steve Byland/SS; 136, kyslynskyy/AD; **Jaguar Cub Cuties:** 137, ZSSD/MP; 138-139, Sergio Pitamitz/NGIC; 140, ZUMA Press Inc/ AL; 141, belizar/SS; 141 (inset), worldswildlifewonders/SS; 142-143, Nick Gordon/NPL; 144-145, blickwinkel/AL; 146, Steve Winter/ NGIC; 147, Nick Hawkins/NPL; 148, Nick Gordon/NPL; 149, Janet Horton/Danita Delimont/AD; 150, ZSSD/MP; 151, Jeff Foott/GI; 152-153, Marc Moritsch/NGIC; 154, Shattil & Rozinski/NPL; **Manatee Man to the Rescue:** 155, Jamal A. Galves/Clearwater Marine Aquarium Research Institute; 156, Jon Arnold Images Ltd/ AL; 157, 158, Jamal A. Galves/Clearwater Marine Aquarium Research Institute; 159, imageBROKER/AL; 160-171, Jamal A. Galves/Clearwater Marine Aquarium Research Institute; 172, Tim Fitzharris/MP; **A Panda Cub Grows Up:** 173, Xinhua/AL; 174-175, Chris Stenger/Buiten-beeld/MP; 176, Gavin Maxwell/NPL; 177, Katherine Feng/MP; 178, Eric Baccega/NPL; 179, Xinhua/AL; 180-181, Katherine Feng/MP; 182, Suzi Eszterhas/MP; 183, National Geographic Channel/NGIC; 184, Ami Vitale/NGIC; 185, Robert Harding Picture Library/NGIC; 186, Katherine Feng/MP; 187, Robert Harding Picture Library/NGIC; 188-189, 190, Jak Wonderly/ NGIC; **A Baby Bobcat: Lost Then Found:** 191, Discover Wildcare; 192, Sundry Photography/GI; 193, Melanie Piazza/WildCare; 194-195, 196, Melanie Piazza/Discover Wildcare; 197, Melanie Piazza/ WildCare; 198-199, 200, Melanie Piazza/Discover Wildcare; 201, Alison Hermance/WildCare; 202-207, Sierra Wildlife Rescue; **Back Matter:** 208, Suzi Eszterhas/MP